10-WEEK TRUTH-IN-TESTIMONY STUDY

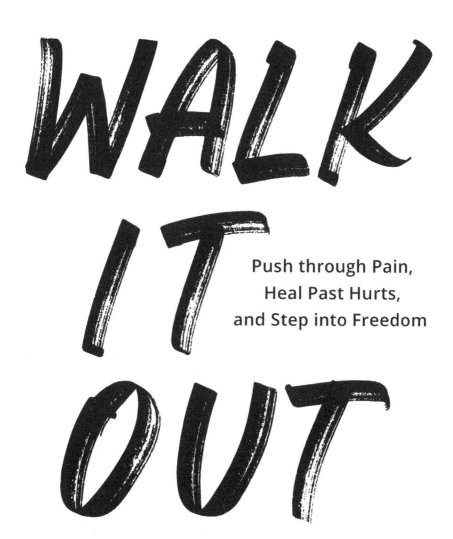

WALK IT OUT

Push through Pain,
Heal Past Hurts,
and Step into Freedom

AMY S. DUDLEY

Walk It Out: Push through Pain, Heal Past Hurts, and Step into Freedom

Copyright © 2021 by Amy Dudley

Unless otherwise noted, all scriptures are from the THE HOLY BIBLE, NEW INTERNATIONAL VERSION®, NIV® Copyright © 1973, 1978, 1984, 2011 by Biblica, Inc.® Used by permission. All rights reserved worldwide.

Scripture quotations marked (ESV) are from the ESV® Bible (The Holy Bible, English Standard Version®), copyright © 2001 by Crossway, a publishing ministry of Good News Publishers. Used by permission. All rights reserved.

Scripture quotations marked (NKJV) taken from the New King James Version®. Copyright © 1982 by Thomas Nelson. Used by permission. All rights reserved.

Scripture quotations marked (NASB) taken from the (NASB®) New American Standard Bible®, Copyright © 1960, 1971, 1977, 1995, 2020 by The Lockman Foundation. Used by permission. All rights reserved. www.lockman.org.

Scripture quotations marked (TPT) are from The Passion Translation®. Copyright © 2017, 2018 by Passion & Fire Ministries, Inc. Used by permission. All rights reserved. ThePassionTranslation.com.

Scripture quotations marked (NLT) are taken from the Holy Bible, New Living Translation, copyright ©1996, 2004, 2015 by Tyndale House Foundation. Used by permission of Tyndale House Publishers, Carol Stream, Illinois 60188. All rights reserved.

Publishing and Design Services: MelindaMartin.me
Editor: Beth Lottig

ISBN: 979-8-9850785-0-3 (paperback), 979-8-9850785-1-0 (epub)

Printed in the United States of America

DEDICATED TO

my inspiring kids, Alex, Sam, Max, and Lilly,
and to my amazing parents, John & Kathy.

Thank you for continuing to teach me to put one foot in front
of the other. I pray you walk fearlessly by faith all the days
of your life, experiencing all there is for you to the fullest.
Capture the moments. Never stop walking. Your story matters.

"For we walk by faith, not by sight."
—2 Corinthians 5:7 (ESV)

CONTENTS

INTRODUCTION

"For we walk by faith, not by sight" (2 Corinthians 5:7, ESV) is my life verse. It's also the first verse I memorized in the Bible ten years ago when I opened it for the first time. I attended a private Christian school, but we didn't read the Bible. We memorized prayers, took theology classes, and attended mass weekly. All provided a fantastic foundation. For as long as I can remember, I've been searching for more. Just ask my mom.

In this book, I walk out my early life experiences one step at a time. I'm not sure about you, but I tend to get off balance if I'm not paying attention. (Ha ha.) It's been that way since I was a little girl! Writing this book has helped me get out of my own way, and I pray my stories do the same for you.

The *Walk It Out* devotional is designed to open communication within your family and circle of friends through stories, reflection, and questions. I pray you find deeper intimacy and healing in your relationships throughout these pages.

HERE'S THE SKINNY

There are ten weeks in total and content for each day of the week. The daily sections are snippets from my childhood experiences, preschool through high school. These stories are hysterical, heartbreaking, and everything in between. All true. I am open, vulnerable, and real. There is truth in testimony.

At the end of each day, there are three questions. I encourage you to pause and answer each of them to "walk " deeper. Close your eyes, be still, and ask Jesus what HE wants you to know. Where was Jesus in your memory? What was Jesus doing? What negative emotion are you feeling? Write it down on your paper. Imagine handing your paper to Jesus. What does Jesus do with your paper? Who does Jesus say you are? Write your true identity down. The truth Jesus reveals about who HE says you are will not only allow you to freely walk in your true identity, who HE created you to be, but will heal you from the inside out.

Breathe in the simple prayer per day, and I double dog dare you to share your daily prayer with someone else. Say it, text it, post it. You do you. Walk it out.

There is a special note from God and a Bible story during the week. Each week ends with a longer prayer followed by declarations, which can be torn out as reminders of who God says you are. I boldly say again, "Tag, you're it! Receive, copy, paste, share, post, and do it again."

Read slow, fast, one day or week at a time. You choose the best pace for you to reap all that has been sown from front to back. Last but not least, there is one Bible memory verse per week separated by day to help with memorization. By the end of the book, you'll have not one, but ten Bible verses memorized! How cool is that?

I can't wait to *Walk It Out* with you. Let's turn the page and dive in!

P.S. Jesus gets all the credit. He walks it out with me daily.

WEEK 1

I HAVE YOU

MEMORY VERSE

"Have I not commanded you?
Be strong and courageous.
Do not be terrified; do not be discouraged,
for the Lord your God will be with you wherever you go."

—JOSHUA 1:9

DAY 1

HAVE I NOT COMMANDED YOU...

My dad loves to play toilet dunking. You have never heard of it before? Without warning, one of us kids gets picked up, turned upside down, and tickled. Everyone but Mom is laughing and screaming uncontrollably. Mom does not like this game.

Daddy carries me to the nearest bathroom. My siblings are jumping up and down, yelling, "Do it, do it, do it!"

"Should I flush you down the toilet today?"

"NOOOOO!" I yell, laughing hysterically.

"Are you sure?"

"YES, I'm SURE!"

"Yes, you're sure you want me to flush you away?"

"Nooo—I mean no, don't flush me down there!"

My brother and sister yell, "YES, do it this time!"

Daddy replies, "I couldn't flush you away because you're too special." He pretends to drop me closer to the water until I say, "You win!"

He places me on my feet, looks me in the eyes, and says with a giant hug, "I have you. I love you. You're staying right here."

WALK DEEPER

1. What are your favorite games to play? _____

   _____

   _____

2. Do you like following rules? Why or why not? _____

   _____

   _____

3. How does God have you? Explain. _____

   _____

   _____

MEMORY VERSE

"Have I not commanded you?
Be strong and courageous.
Do not be terrified; do not be discouraged,
for the Lord your God will be with you wherever you go."

—JOSHUA 1:9

I pray to follow your commandments, in Jesus' name, Amen.

DAY 2

BE STRONG...

The oldest of three kids, I am quiet, compliant, shy, and fearful—yet strong. My siblings say I am a bossy mother hen who hates losing and has to be first. They are not wrong.

I look out for them and do my share of chores. I get blamed for countless shenanigans. *You are the oldest and should know better.*

I want to fit in. I crave friends and to be included, but I am awkward and different. I am not sure why because I feel confident and safe at home.

As soon as I step outside of my family comfort zone, I freeze. Why can't I speak up? I want to join others and play. If words happen to form, they are but a whisper and fall to the ground. It is easier to quietly drift away daydreaming than rely on my hidden strength.

I watch other kids, overhear their conversations, but pretend I do not. I am very aware of what is happening around me but feel invisible.

My escape spot is my favorite swing in the backyard. I am free. I soar through the air pumping my legs, pretending to touch the sky. I close my eyes, squealing with joy and confidence.

No talking, just thinking. No doing, just being. No expectations. Simply flowing. Listening. What is this peace that comforts my soul?

WALK DEEPER

1. Do you have siblings or cousins? Share. _____

   _____

   _____

2. Where do you feel most peaceful? _____

   _____

   _____

3. What strengths did God give you to focus on? _____

   _____

   _____

MEMORY VERSE

"Have I not commanded you?
Be strong and courageous.
Do not be terrified; do not be discouraged,
for the Lord your God will be with you wherever you go."

—JOSHUA 1:9

> *I pray I have supernatural strength today*
> *and every day, in Jesus' name, Amen.*

DAY 3

AND COURAGEOUS . . .

Safety Town. When is Mom returning to pick me up? I am practicing crossing crosswalks, waiting at traffic lights, learning signs.

I am pretending to drive a plastic car like my big wheel at home. *This makes no sense. I want to go home. Why do I have to do this?*

I cannot focus. I am doing what they ask. But I'm doing it the wrong way. I do not understand this. *Why am I here? I did the best I could. Wasn't that good enough?*

I repeat: "Green light means go, yellow means wait, and red means stop."

"Pay attention, little girl!"

"Look at me. Look to your right and left."

"You can't just stand or sit there; take a step!"

I do not want to be here. *When will this be over?*

Mom returns, and now I can breathe. The ride home is silent. She will not look at me. Her brow is wrinkled. I do not like when she is mad. I wish we could talk about what happened. She was not there.

I got a bad report. Mom is frustrated.

"You knew I was coming back. I always do. I don't under-stand," she lectures.

I drift off. *Why do I feel so different? I am a good girl. I follow directions. Does anyone hear or see me? Things are so fast.*

WALK DEEPER

1. Do you remember a time when you experienced fear?
    Share._____

    _____

    _____

2. Imagine a piece of paper showing your feelings and thoughts
    from this fearful event. What does your paper say? _____

    _____

    _____

3. Visualize Jesus. Where is Jesus during the event? Hand
    him your imaginary paper. What did Jesus do with your
    paper? Who does Jesus say you are? How does God
    have you? HINT: Ask HIM and share._____

    _____

    _____

MEMORY VERSE

"Have I not commanded you?
Be strong and courageous.
Do not be terrified; do not be discouraged,
for the Lord your God will be with you wherever you go."

—JOSHUA 1:9

I pray for an increase in courage, in Jesus' name, Amen.

DAY 4

DO NOT BE TERRIFIED . . .

I fold laundry, put away dishes, set the table, brush my teeth most days, make my bed, pick weeds, and care for my brother and sister. I play school. I host tea parties—just me, my teddy bear, and my dolls.

I love to play dress-up in Mom's closet. What girl does not? I am bold when I dress up. I look just like her! I do have confidence.

ESTHER

There was a young woman in the Bible named Esther. She would have loved to play dress-up like her mother, but she was an orphan being raised by her uncle Mordecai.

Mordecai told Esther to keep her real name, Hadassah, and her Jewish lineage a secret until the right time. Esther was beautiful, and she was forced to live in the palace for a year, along with many other girls, to prepare to be introduced to King Ahasuerus. She also had to keep a giant secret of who she was. Esther had to be bold and did not have a choice.

When the year was over, the king ended up choosing Esther, declared her queen, and set the royal crown on her head!

Soon after, Queen Esther was made aware of an evil plot against her people, the Jews, by her husband's right-hand man, Haman. The king did not know he was a bad man. Esther was afraid, yet knew she had to do something.

She fasted and prayed for three days along with her people. She got dressed up and went to see the king all by herself. Queen Esther could have been killed for asking to meet with him without being invited.

Esther courageously shared her secret and told the truth about who she was, then boldly begged the king to spare her people. The king found out about Haman and his evil plan. He was so mad he ordered Haman to be hanged on the gallows he originally built for her cousin Mordecai. Haman's pride and cruelty had led to his destruction.

Esther was so brave—she saved her people. In the end, Esther told the truth about who she was and did not pretend to be anyone else, even if it meant she would be killed. God used her for such a time to save His chosen people.

God has a purpose and plan for me. I like me and do not want to be anyone else! I can be strong and brave.

WALK DEEPER

1. Have you ever pretended to be someone else? _____
   _____
   _____

2. Share a time you had to have courage. _____
   _____
   _____

3. Has God ever asked you to be brave like Esther? _____
   _____
   _____

MEMORY VERSE

"Have I not commanded you?
Be strong and courageous.
Do not be terrified; do not be discouraged,
for the Lord your God will be with you wherever you go."

—JOSHUA 1:9

I pray and boldly ask for an Esther anointing, in Jesus' name, Amen.

DAY 5

DO NOT BE DISCOURAGED...

I'm struggling in school. Mom's on a mission for me to fit in, get good grades, and be like other kids. *What does that mean?*

Mom's face says it all.

"We recommend she repeat first grade," my teachers say. Mom disagrees.

The words Daddy says after toilet dunking—*I have you. I love you. You're staying right here*—are on repeat in my head.

I overhear Mom talking to Dad: "No one is going to tell me my daughter needs to be held back. They do not know her. They do not know me. We'll pay for summer school, work with her, and we'll show them."

Mom's a fighter. Persistent.

"Why do I have to go to summer school, Mom? No one else has to!"

"We have to get you caught up in some areas."

"But I don't want to!"

"You don't have a choice."

And so it begins. Striving to understand numbers, reading, telling time. To prove what? That I am not dumb. Normal. Prove to whom? Family, friends, teachers? Fitting in is exhausting.

WALK DEEPER

1. Does learning come easy for you? What is hard for you?

   _____

   _____

2. How do you feel loved? Do you need to earn love to feel loved?_____

   _____

3. How does God help you when you are discouraged? Share._____

   _____

   _____

MEMORY VERSE

"Have I not commanded you?
Be strong and courageous.
Do not be terrified; do not be discouraged,
for the Lord your God will be with you wherever you go."

—JOSHUA 1:9

> *Thank you for reminding me I always fit in with you, God,*
> *in Jesus' name, Amen.*

DAY 6

FOR THE LORD YOUR GOD WILL BE . . .

Can I just go out and swing? Ms. Delores is a miserable summer tutor. My lack of skill annoys her. I cannot focus. She crosses her arms, glaring at me. I dread seeing giant red X's and hearing her say, "Do it again."

Shoot, even the clock would run away if it could. It is dismal.

Ms. Delores does not want to be there. Neither do I. At least we agree on something. It is summer. Not school. I wonder if she even likes being a teacher.

If I become a teacher, I will encourage students just like me. Help them feel proud. It is not about getting it right or wrong but showing up. Doing the absolute best. Who cares how many times it takes to understand?

At least that is what I tell my stuffed animals. I am smart. I show up, even when I have no idea what is going on. I will put shameful summer school red marks behind me.

NOTE FROM GOD

I do have YOU. Just put one foot in front of the other, and I will help you do it again. Look past the red marks on your paper. I am using this to raise you up, but I cannot refine you unless you go through the battle.

I will never leave you or forsake you, ever (Hebrews 13:5).

I have you,

God

WALK DEEPER

1. When have you had to *"do it again"* or repeat something?

    _____

    _____

    _____

2. Do you encourage others? How?_____

    _____

    _____

3. How does God help you and have you when you are
    afraid? _____

    _____

    _____

MEMORY VERSE

"Have I not commanded you?
Be strong and courageous.
Do not be terrified; do not be discouraged,
for the Lord your God will be with you wherever you go."

—JOSHUA 1:9

I pray discouragement never holds me back, in Jesus' name, Amen.

DAY 7

WITH YOU WHEREVER YOU GO...

Recess—it's where older, bigger kids love to torture the nice, quiet ones. Have you ever been bullied? Me too. It never stops. Poking. Hair pulling. Horrible name-calling.

The torment is real. But it's hidden when teachers, parent volunteers, or bus drivers are not looking. Mom tells me she has eyes on the back of her head. No one else seems to. How could she be the only one?

Other students do not stand up for me. *Cowards*. I would. I know what it feels like to not have help.

Mom and Dad talk to school administrators. Even the bully's parents. He lives a few streets over.

"Walk away," Mom and Dad recommend.

"But he follows me!"

"Ignore him. Eventually, it will stop."

Have you ever had a defining moment? Me too. Everything changes. I became a superhero, not knowing I could without changing clothes.

I will never forget riding home. The bully is seated behind me on the bus, hitting the back of my seat with his knees. Nonstop.

I leap to my feet, glaring into his eyes and scream, "Leave me alone!" I slap him across the face. My hand stings.

Time stops. Seconds seem like years. Both of us are stunned. I slide back in my seat. *Where did that come from? Why now?* My heart pounds outside of my chest. *What have I done?* My mind races a thousand miles per hour. *I am in so much trouble. Mom is going to kill me! What was I thinking?*

My bus driver, Mr. Gus, forever becomes my hero. I glance and see him staring at me in his rearview mirror. He winks, clenches his right fist, mouthing, "Thatta girl!"

I let out a sigh of relief and sit taller with my shoulders back. As I get off the bus, he whispers, "I am so proud of you. This stays between us."

The bullying stops. For the first time, I realize *I am brave. I am strong. I have a voice.*

WALK DEEPER

1. Have you ever been bullied or picked on, or have you been the bully? Share. _____

    _____

    _____

2. Who protects or stands up for you? Do you have a hero?

    _____

    _____

    _____

3. How does God help you? How do you know God is for you?

    _____

    _____

    _____

MEMORY VERSE

"Have I not commanded you?
Be strong and courageous.
Do not be terrified; do not be discouraged,
for the Lord your God will be with you wherever you go."

—JOSHUA 1:9

I pray to walk where you have walked, in Jesus' name, Amen.

I HAVE YOU

PRAYER

Father, I will let go. I am strong. I am boldly taking one step at a time. Thank you for having me right where I am, even in my weakness—in a game, at school, my bedroom, the playground; on the bus, with bullies, family, teachers; while learning, swinging, finishing chores, or dressing up. You are right by my side. You have me covered, just like Esther, busily working behind the scenes. Thank you for going before me. Thank you for allowing me to walk where you have. You are with me wherever I go, directing and prospering my steps (Proverbs 16:9). I am your bold, brave queen. I trust you.

Your sold-out daughter

Sweet Daughter, I have you. I love you. I am right here hugging you.

Your forever loving daddy,

God

I HAVE YOU

DECLARATIONS FROM GOD

I have you in my arms.
I have you while you are silent.
I have you while you are sleeping.
I have you throughout your day.
I have you when you are sad, happy, and mad.
I have you when you are busy.
I have you when you are thinking.
I have you when you are waiting.
I have you when you are coming and going.
I have you when you are afraid.
I have you when you think you are alone.
I have you when you are hurt.
I have you always and forever.
I have you, and you have me.

WEEK 2

I SEE YOU

MEMORY VERSE

"So we fix our eyes not on what is seen,
but on what is unseen,
since what is seen is temporary,
but what is unseen is eternal."

—2 CORINTHIANS 4:18

DAY 1

SO WE FIX OUR EYES . . .

I have a secret that embarrasses me, one that no one knows about because my hair covers it. I was born this way. My secret is insignificant to others, but it crushes me.

I am always worried someone is going to make fun of me, like in Safety Town or summer school. I could not drive the plastic car, tell time, or count. Now it is a few years later, and I still feel different. I cannot figure out why.

Other kids are reading stories and playing games together. I am comforted by swinging on my swing set alone in my backyard. I am barely double digits and not sure how long not fitting in lasts. Maybe I will fit in next week, year—or never.

My secret cannot change, but I wonder if anyone else has a secret. I am not throwing a pity party for myself. I will not let my thoughts pull me down. That's easier said than done. God never promises easy but says all things with Him are possible. He sees my treasured secrets.

WALK DEEPER

1. Is there something you do not want anyone to know about? _____

    _____

    _____

2. Do you see what others see about you, and vice versa? Share._____

    _____

    _____

3. What is God telling you about your thoughts? _____

    _____

    _____

MEMORY VERSE

"So we fix our eyes not on what is seen, but on what is unseen, since what is seen is temporary, but what is unseen is eternal."

—2 CORINTHIANS 4:18

> *I pray to fix my eyes on you, God, in Jesus' name, Amen.*

DAY 2
NOT ON WHAT IS SEEN...

A boy sitting behind me pokes his pencil repeatedly at my birthmark, a bald spot on the back of my head. He thinks it is funny, but it is devastating to me.

I was born with a cyst the size of my thumbnail. Mom said it happened because I was thrashing in the birth canal. Thankfully, it is not serious.

Still, the back of my head feels like a giant blinking light, flashing repeatedly: SHE IS DIFFERENT.

Marked.

Mom and I do our best to cover it up. Like Rudolph, though, it never fails to reappear. Next come questions, giggling, and jokes. I pretend not to care, but the words crush me.

I think maybe part of my brain got sucked out. That is why I cannot tell time, count money, read, or understand math. Think about it! Maybe this is why others breeze through school while I struggle.

NOTE FROM GOD

Sweet girl, you are my fearless, beloved royal daughter, princess warrior, and you were born for such a time as this (Esther 4:14). You just do not know it yet. Trust me—not what you see. I formed you perfectly in your mother's womb, numbering every hair on your head (Luke 12:7).

I love and adore you,

God

WALK DEEPER

1. Do you have a special birthmark, scar, freckle, mole, or mark? Share. How does this make you feel? _____

   _____

   _____

2. What do others see in you that you do not see in yourself? Explain. _____

   _____

   _____

3. What do you think Jesus sees in you? _____

   _____

   _____

MEMORY VERSE

"So we fix our eyes not on what is seen, but on what is unseen, since what is seen is temporary, but what is unseen is eternal."

—2 CORINTHIANS 4:18

I pray people see the Jesus in me, in Jesus' name, Amen.

DAY 3

BUT ON WHAT IS UNSEEN . . .

As if the spot on my head was not enough, I was also born pigeon-toed. Are you kidding me?! Another secret. Apparently, I waddled like a duck with my toes pointing in when I was a baby. Both legs had to be casted to correct it. Phew! Thankfully, I can walk in elementary school without tripping myself!

I can tell this was not easy for my parents. They say I rarely cried but did not sleep much. When I look at pictures, I see a good little girl but feel sad for her. That must have been uncomfortable lying in the same position all the time. I am glad I do not remember.

I can't stand wearing my boring white clunky old lady orthopedic tie shoes (say that ten times fast—ha). So ugly. I need support so my feet do not turn back in. On the bright side, my shoes take attention off my bald spot. Still awkward though.

No one knows why I was born with a cyst and pigeon toes, but God does. *Why can't I be like everyone else?* Hey, wait—I do not want to be anyone else! I just want to be me.

God sees me as special, and no one else can be me. I have treasures right in front of me, like my family, food, clothes, house, bed, teddy bear, and more. I do not want to turn away or close my eyes to protect myself.

Eyes, stay open and focused on the good things.

WALK DEEPER

1. Are there any other secrets you forgot about? _____
    _____
    _____

2. What do you love about yourself? Share. _____
    _____
    _____

3. What treasures did God give you? _____
    _____
    _____

MEMORY VERSE

"So we fix our eyes not on what is seen, but on what is unseen, since what is seen is temporary, but what is unseen is eternal."

—2 CORINTHIANS 4:18

Thank you for creating me special, in Jesus' name, Amen.

DAY 4

SINCE WHAT IS SEEN...

The popular girls invite me to a sleepover! All day, I skip from class to class in my ugly orthopedic shoes, feeling the joy of being included.

While I'm getting my bookbag in our classroom lockers at the end of the day, one of the girls pulls me aside and whispers, "Can I talk to you? The invitation is not real. You are not invited. We wanted to see what you would do."

I spend the bus ride home thinking about what happened. I am invited and uninvited—on the same day. I run off the bus breathless to tell Mom. I still cannot believe it. Girls asked me over for a sleepover and I said yes! But then they told me I was not invited.

Mom asks, "What did you do?"

"Oh, I knew that!" I say, playing it off cool. I am confused on the inside because I *did not* know. Mom seems sad.

I walk away quietly to my bedroom. At least the girls knew my name. They talked to me.

I am not unseen. Poor Mom is sad.

WALK DEEPER

1.   Have you ever experienced being left out? Do you include others? _____

_____

_____

2.   Do you feel seen or unseen by people? What does Jesus see?_____

_____

_____

3.   Can you hear God whispering to you? Share. _____

_____

_____

MEMORY VERSE

"So we fix our eyes not on what is seen, but on what is unseen, since what is seen is temporary, but what is unseen is eternal."

—2 CORINTHIANS 4:18

I pray to see the Jesus in others, in Jesus' name, Amen.

DAY 5

IS TEMPORARY . . .

The first day after spring break is awful. All I can think about is jumping waves, playing paddleball on the beach, and time with family.

I did not miss school, classmates, or homework during the break, but I am excited to give my teacher a gift—a bag of oranges from Florida.

Miss Romano is fun and nice to me. Except today. She knows I am not paying attention. I'm daydreaming, and she calls my name. Busted. I have no idea what she is teaching.

Dangling participle . . . what is that? I'm standing at the blackboard in front of my class clueless, face red with embarrassment. Miss Romano asks me to sit down, saying when I am ready, I can participate in class.

I am still thinking about this on my way home on the bus. Now I am in the kitchen talking to Mom.

"How was your day?" asks Mom.

"Great!"

"Did Miss Romano like the oranges you gave her?"

"Nope."

"Really? Why?"

"I didn't give them to her," I say, as I am putting them on the counter. "I have changed my mind. Miss Romano doesn't deserve them."

I know I was wrong. I should have been listening in class and following directions. I made a mistake. We all do. Miss Romano did not need to embarrass me. I never make fun of her like other kids. I still forgive her.

"Oranges for dinner, everyone!"

MIRIAM

In the Bible, there is a girl named Miriam. She was the older sister to Moses and played an important role in the Exodus of the Jews from Egypt. Unfortunately, her pride got her in trouble. She did not see this at all. As a baby, Moses' mom put him in a basket and sent him down a river to save his life. It is likely Miriam watched over baby Moses as he floated down the river (read Exodus 2:4). Pharaoh's daughter found him. Miriam intervened, offering her mom to nurse and help raise him in the palace. Later, God chose Moses to lead the Israelites out of slavery in Egypt, and Miriam was there to help! Miriam was like all of us. She had some great qualities, but she also had some unfavorable qualities. Miriam was loving and protective of her baby brother. And she was a leader. She wrote a beautiful song women would sing to say thanks to God for rescuing them. But Miriam had a problem with complaining (read Numbers 12). She complained about Moses' leadership and even the woman he married. Maybe Miriam was jealous Moses was in charge and she was not? She probably felt unseen. God did not like Miriam complaining. Despite Miriam's problems, God still used her, and He can use us, even when we have bad days. God sees everything.

———————

I am sorry, God. My pride got in the way. I should have told the truth. Forgive me for complaining about Miss Romano. Okay—and about school, chores, homework, and more. I see now the oranges may have brightened her day.

WALK DEEPER

1.   Are you a complainer? What do you complain about? Why?_____

     _____

     _____

2.   What do you do when you are embarrassed?_____

     _____

     _____

3.   You deserve God's love. How do you know? Share. _____

     _____

     _____

MEMORY VERSE

"So we fix our eyes not on what is seen, but on what is unseen, since what is seen is temporary, but what is unseen is eternal."

—2 CORINTHIANS 4:18

I pray you use me all the time, God, in Jesus' name, Amen.

DAY 6

BUT WHAT IS UNSEEN...

cannot rock slip-on shoes like the cool kids. I still try, but I end up walking barefoot every time. So embarrassing.

It's time for new school shoes, and I choose navy Converse tie tennis shoes. Mom tries to talk me out of them, but I insist. "I'm doing it, along with knee-high socks!" This combo will go perfect with my school uniform. I am tired of trying to be like everyone else. We already dress alike. Mom finally agrees. I am excited to wear these fun tie shoes!

Even though I get pulled out of class for extra help, at least I can walk by everyone in my unique style.

On top of being different, I continue to see what others do not see. It makes me feel bad seeing teachers' eyes rolling, kids whispering, passing notes, throwing spitballs, and cheating. Nothing escapes my notice. I wish what I see would not bother me so much.

WALK DEEPER

1. Do you love shoes? What are your favorites and why?

    _____

    _____

    _____

2. What qualities in you draw attention to you? Share.

    _____

    _____

    _____

3. What does God notice about you? What do you notice
    about God? _____

    _____

    _____

MEMORY VERSE

"So we fix our eyes not on what is seen, but on what is unseen,
since what is seen is temporary, but what is unseen is eternal."

—2 CORINTHIANS 4:18

> *I pray to not get distracted by what I see in others,*
> *in Jesus' name, Amen.*

DAY 7

IS ETERNAL...

Mom realizes I cannot read road signs until we pass them. I did not know. The blackboard is kind of blurry, but I can see it.

I try on glasses for the first time. A light switch flips on, and a crisp, colorful, bright new world opens right before my eyes. I am so excited! The difference is night and day.

But now my classmates, mostly boys, call me "four eyes." Everyone wearing glasses gets this name.

They can call me four eyes all they want. I love my new glasses. I feel like a brand new me because I can see! I see little and big things, close and far away. It is like a giant coloring book came to life. Even when my teacher is across the room writing on the board, I can see. I never knew this could happen. I just woke up from a lifelong nap.

Welcome to the party.

NOTE FROM GOD

You are not a mistake. I made you different on purpose, including your crooked legs, bald spot, four eyes, and more. Stop trying to cover up and change who I purposely designed you to be. You belong. Can you trust me?

Yes, Lord. But . . . I cannot see you.

Yes, you can. Close your eyes. What do you see?

I see grassy fields, blue skies, and the two of us dancing effortlessly without touching the ground.

Isn't it amazing?

Yes. Invigorating.

Carry this with you all day. Flow with Me all day so we can bring your "scribbles" and goof-ups to life!

WALK DEEPER

1. What do you see when your eyes are open and closed? Share._____

   _____

   _____

2. Do you look for God? When, where, and how? _____

   _____

   _____

3. How does God help you see what HE sees in you? _____

   _____

   _____

MEMORY VERSE

"So we fix our eyes not on what is seen, but on what is unseen, since what is seen is temporary, but what is unseen is eternal."

—2 CORINTHIANS 4:18

God help me to see what you see, in Jesus' name I pray, Amen.

I SEE YOU

PRAYER

You will reveal the full story someday. Until then, you see me and my heart. Thank you for opening my eyes and making me unique. Thank you for making me a leader like Miriam. Forgive me when I complain or am not nice when I know better. God, thank you. I have a place at the table with you. I am always invited and included, no matter my sock color, shoes, mistakes, marks, mean girls, or if I like oranges or not. Father, I come before you to see all you have for me. I want to enjoy your fruit. Help me not to be blinded to your truths and fullness. I ask you to open the eyes of my heart to your truths and to the fullness of who you are. Help others to see you in me and help me to see you in them. I love you.

Love,

Your focused, spunky, magnetic leader girl

Sweet Daughter, I see you. I see your heart. I adore you and am so proud of you. I am right here watching you.

Your forever loving daddy,

God

I SEE YOU

DECLARATIONS FROM GOD

I see your heart.
I see your pain.
I see when you are lost.
I see your troubles.
I see the light in you.
I see the warrior in you.
I see your temptations.
I see you choosing me.
I see you dreaming bigger.
I see your faith growing.
I see your destiny.
I see you multiplying.
I see you watching.
I see you leading my people.

WEEK 3

I HEAR YOU

MEMORY VERSE

"And your ears shall hear a word behind you, saying,
'This is the way, walk in it,' when you turn to the right or
when you turn to the left."

—ISAIAH 30:21 (ESV)

DAY 1

AND YOUR EARS...

I have remained off the bullying grid, but I still do not have many friends. I am more comfortable with school and routines. I am not comfortable with upcoming body changes. I can hear classmates talking nonstop.

Everyone is transforming while my chest is flat as a board, armpits smooth, and nothing down below. Phew. These upcoming changes are constantly on my mind. "What size are you? Did you get 'it' yet?" girls ask. When will I say, "Yes, me too"?

I beg Mom for a training bra. She is laughing out loud, but I persist. The next thing I know, Grandma and I are at the store. Bra shopping. I can hear her trying not to laugh.

WALK DEEPER

1. What do you love about your body? _____
   _____
   _____

2. Is there anything you do not like or fear about your body? Why? _____
   _____
   _____

3. God hears your thoughts! What does God want you to hear? _____
   _____
   _____

MEMORY VERSE

"And your ears shall hear a word behind you, saying,
'This is the way, walk in it,' when you turn to the right or
when you turn to the left."

—ISAIAH 30:21 (ESV)

I pray to love every part of my body, in Jesus' name, Amen.

DAY 2

SHALL HEAR A WORD...

Mom hires her friend's daughter to prepare me for tryouts. *Excuse me, what?* Cheerleading is not even on my radar. Who is this girl, Lisa?

She cheers for the most competitive high school team in town. I'm in middle school, and full panic has set in. First, I will have to use my voice. I don't even know what that sounds like. I talk at home, but in front of others at school? No way.

Second, I must make up a routine. Where do I even begin? Duh, it's why Mom hired Lisa. I am already shaking, thinking about standing in front of judges. My memorizing skills stink.

I must shout and move at the same time. They may see me but will never hear me. This seems impossible. I do not want to do this.

I have two left feet.

A cheerleader? In front of people? No thank you. Besides, Lisa is probably a popular, perfect, included girl. Even if she likes me, she will end up frustrated like everyone else.

WALK DEEPER

1. Do you have a mentor or coach? Are you teachable?

   _____

   _____

   _____

2. Do you make assumptions about others? Explain.

   _____

   _____

   _____

3. What do you hear in your head when God introduces new adventures?_____

   _____

   _____

MEMORY VERSE

"And your ears shall hear a word behind you, saying,
'This is the way, walk in it,' when you turn to the right or
when you turn to the left."

—ISAIAH 30:21 (ESV)

> *I pray I can say yes to new things without fear,*
> *in Jesus' name, Amen.*

DAY 3

BEHIND YOU, SAYING...

This whole cheerleading thing is giving me kindergarten dance recital flashbacks. I did not want to dance, but I was not allowed to quit. "You need to finish what you start," my mom says.

I attempted something new and quickly learned dance was not for me. I could hear kids tapping left when I was tapping right. Off-beat tapping is the worst sound.

I practiced over and over and over for weeks, hoping recital day would never come. It did. I was dressed up in an expensive tutu, blinded by stage lights, and scared to death.

I forgot the entire routine and could not move—frozen in front of the entire audience. I wish I could erase the memory. Ugh.

I want to be heard. I said I would never do anything like that again. Mom doesn't talk to me for days. She is so mad at me. I don't want Mom to be mad again if I mess up cheerleading tryouts. *Why doesn't anyone listen to me?*

WALK DEEPER

1.   Is the silent treatment or yelling worse? Both produce scars. _____

     _____

     _____

2.   Do you say yes to please people, so you do not disappoint them? _____

     _____

     _____

3.   Where is God when you are offbeat or off track? _____

     _____

     _____

MEMORY VERSE

"And your ears shall hear a word behind you, saying,
'This is the way, walk in it,' when you turn to the right or
when you turn to the left."

—ISAIAH 30:21 (ESV)

I pray to please you, God, above everything, in Jesus' name, Amen.

DAY 4

THIS IS THE WAY ...

" Tap was then; this is now. You're trying out, and you *will* make the cheer squad," says Mom. She knows I do not have many friends.

The declaration is made. I have no escape tactics. Mom is tired of secret playground drive-bys in her car when she sees me all by myself every day during recess. Mom admits she does it weekly, watching me pitifully attempt to hide in corners not to be seen, heard, or picked last for kickball. Thank God I have never seen her.

The only reason I am chosen for kickball is because there are not enough players. I can hear the kids whispering behind my back. I wish someone would listen to me.

"Not her. She cannot kick the ball or run fast," they whisper behind their hands. "We are going to lose if she's on our team. You take her—you have the best players and can make up for her."

I want to yell, "You know I can hear you, right?" I do not.

WALK DEEPER

1. How do you respond when you do not have a choice?

    _____
    _____
    _____

2. What do you do when others whisper about you? _____

    _____
    _____

3. Does God show you the way to go? How?_____

    _____
    _____

MEMORY VERSE

"And your ears shall hear a word behind you, saying,
'This is the way, walk in it,' when you turn to the right or
when you turn to the left."

—ISAIAH 30:21 (ESV)

> *I pray I hear you clearly, God, so I know your way,
> in Jesus' name, Amen.*

DAY 5

WALK IN IT...

For weeks, I have been practicing cheerleading routines. I have no choice. Mom's adamant. But I start to notice my confidence growing. I stand a little straighter and make mistakes less often. *Mom may be right about this.*

Lisa is patient and kind. Forgive me for thinking the worst. She explains everything until I understand. Posture, eye contact, project voice, smile, breathe.

Do it again. (*Sound familiar?*) Better. Try again. Do it in front of the mirror. Do you see what I see? Stand on the other side of the yard. I cannot hear you. Louder.

I am secretly beaming on the inside. I do not say a word to anyone because I am afraid of what they will say. I do not want extra pressure, and some things are better left unsaid. Besides, I know someone might try to talk me out of it. Too late—I am not listening.

I am walking this out.

WALK DEEPER

1. What do you love about learning something new? _____
    _____
    _____

2. Do you like to practice? Share. _____
    _____
    _____

3. How do you think God feels when HE hears your voice?
    What "Lisas" has God sent to help you? _____
    _____
    _____

MEMORY VERSE

"And your ears shall hear a word behind you, saying,
'This is the way, walk in it,' when you turn to the right or
when you turn to the left."

—ISAIAH 30:21 (ESV)

I pray to show up the best I know how, in Jesus' name, Amen.

DAY 6
WHEN YOU TURN TO THE RIGHT...

The school bell rings. Today is the day. So many candidates and not many spots. I can do this. I will not forget or freeze because I am prepared.

I am one of the last to enter the gymnasium. My routine played in my head a thousand times while waiting, but I know I am ready.

Something shifts as I stand in front of three guest judges. I take a deep breath before I begin and pretend I am in the backyard with Lisa. My heart is pounding, and I can hear the blood whooshing through my ears.

As soon as I start, I feel like I am someone else. My mouth is moving, my routine flowing, and my body moving just like we practiced. All eyes are on me, and nothing else is heard but my voice. I am doing it. And I'm doing it right.

I do not miss a beat, nailing every single component from beginning to end. I am shocked and can tell by the judges' faces they are impressed. Mission complete.

I cannot wait to tell Mom and Lisa. I am so proud of myself, no matter the result. I did the best I could, and it feels good. I am awake and alive. *Who am I right now?*

DAVID

The least likely, smallest, and overlooked character in the Bible is David, but the story of David and Goliath is one of the most popular stories (1 Samuel 17). It is a lesson of courage, faith, and overcoming what seems impossible.

David was the youngest of Jesse's twelve sons. One day, the nation of Israel was called to fight the Philistine army that had gathered for war. While David's brothers went to fight, David stayed back to watch the sheep. The two armies gathered to stand on opposite sides of a deep valley. A great Philistine giant named Goliath, who stood over nine feet tall, came to the front of the Philistine battle line each day for forty days and mocked the Israelites and their God. Goliath called them to fight, but King Saul and the Israelites were scared and did nothing.

David was sent by his dad, Jesse, to visit the front lines and bring back battle news from his brothers. David heard Goliath mocking Israel and their God. David was brave and volunteered to fight Goliath. He persuaded King Saul to let him go fight and decided to not wear any of King Saul's armor.

David carried his sling and gathered five smooth stones. Goliath laughed at David, but David responded that even though Goliath had a sword and spear, he came in the name of the Lord Almighty, the God of Israel. David put a rock in his sling and swung one of the rocks at Goliath's head. The rock sank into the giant's forehead, and he fell. David then picked up Goliath's sword and used it to kill Goliath and cut off his head.

The Philistines turned and ran when they saw their giant hero killed. Israel had won the battle because of a boy who had faith and trusted God!

———————

When the day rolled around to try out, I was nervous yet confident in what I practiced. My simple armor consisted of light pink shorts, a striped collared shirt tucked in, bobbysocks, white Keds, and hair pulled back in a ponytail.

For the first time, I experienced courage, boldness, and confidence like David. They heard me. My rhythm was there all along.

WALK DEEPER

1. When have you surprised others and yourself? _____
   _____
   _____

2. What are your Goliaths? _____
   _____
   _____

3. Do you know if you are in sync with God? Explain. _____
   _____
   _____

MEMORY VERSE

"And your ears shall hear a word behind you, saying,
'This is the way, walk in it,' when you turn to the right or
when you turn to the left."

—ISAIAH 30:21 (ESV)

> *I pray to have faith like David, in Jesus' name, Amen.*

DAY 7
OR WHEN YOU TURN TO THE LEFT ...

All candidates are called into the gym to hear the judges' results. Everyone is anxious as names are called one by one. I am counting down the spots left on my fingers.

Everything is a blur when I hear my name. Did they just say what I think they said, or am I hearing things? Everyone is staring at me. *Holy what? I made the squad. Me?*

"Who?" the rest of the candidates mumble. "Her? Really?"

YES, really *really*! For the first time, I did it. I did not want to, but am glad Mom made me. I showed up and delivered a flawless routine, earning a spot on the squad. I am excited to be a part of something I worked hard for. I just punched fear in the face, and it feels great.

The real kicker comes when I quickly realize I am the only one in my grade to make the squad. The rest are older. I was one of few applicants who executed a perfect routine. Practice when no one is looking makes progress.

Overnight, I am elevated to popularity status. Unfortunately, an unexpected price tag of backstabbing and rejection follows. My classmates are jealous because they did not make the squad. Eighth graders are annoyed they must work with me.

Popularity is not what it is cracked up to be. I thought class-mates would celebrate with me. I am wrong. This is so confusing. I would have been happy for them if I did not make it.

I am still not accepted. I feel alone.

A NOTE FROM GOD

A boy no one knew, named David, killed Goliath. Without armor, using only a slingshot and five smooth stones (1 Samuel 17:40–51).

Well done, David. If he can, so can you.

Well done, Daughter.

WALK DEEPER

1. How do you respond when you are caught off guard?

   _____

   _____

   _____

2. Is it easy or hard to cheer others on? Why or why not?

   _____

   _____

   _____

3. How do you give God credit? When do you forget? _____

   _____

   _____

MEMORY VERSE

"And your ears shall hear a word behind you, saying,
'This is the way, walk in it,' when you turn to the right or
when you turn to the left."

—ISAIAH 30:21 (ESV)

I pray to support family and friends, in Jesus' name, Amen.

I HEAR YOU

PRAYER

Father, thank you I can overcome my doubts and fears. With you, I can let go of my unbelief. Accepted or not, I hear you. I am kind and strong. I am enough, even though I hear what those around me say. I am listening to the good and ignoring the mean. Help me to not seek people's approval. Help me to fit in. I thank you for walking right by my side. Thank you for speaking through mentors and answering my prayers. It is not how I ever imagined, but I am learning to expect the unexpected. Thank you for reminding me how special I am. You hear me whether I am cheering, studying, or sleeping. You are always whispering to me. Thank you for showing up and showing off while getting the last word. I know I am in progress, and I trust you. Forgive me for the times I have not trusted.

I love you,

Your sweet overcomer

___

Sweet daughter, I do hear you, and you hear me in the silence or shouting, even when you do not think so. I am always talking to you. Receive my words. Thank you for talking to me. Continue to make space for me. Be still so you can hear me. Get quiet. Let go. Close your eyes. What did I say? Write it down. Where am I? I am still sitting here. What am I doing? I am listening.

I can hear you,

God

I HEAR YOU

DECLARATIONS FROM GOD

I hear your voice.
I hear you laughing.
I hear you crying.
I hear you asking.
I hear you tapping.
I hear them whispering.
I hear you worshipping.
I hear you humming, whistling, and singing.
I hear your passion.
I hear your words.
I hear you speaking up.
I hear you responding.
I hear you all the time.
I hear you, and you hear me.

WEEK 4

I KNOW YOU

MEMORY VERSE

"Before I formed you in the womb I knew you,
before you were born I set you apart;
I appointed you as a prophet to the nations."

—JEREMIAH 1:5

DAY 1

BEFORE I FORMED YOU...

P ep rallies are awesome! We gather outside in my former hiding zone—the playground.

We create a semi-circle with our squad in the middle. All eyes are on us. The entire school erupts like a volcano cheering, clapping, and stomping.

We're a symphony of harmony moving in unison, encouraging one another. We wear our colors with pride, and none of us misses a beat. The excitement continues to build.

It's invigorating and so much fun!

WALK DEEPER

1. What do you love to do on a playground? Share.

   _____

   _____

   _____

2. Do you like to be the center of attention? Why or why
   not?_____

   _____

   _____

3. How does God ask you to cheer others on?_____

   _____

   _____

MEMORY VERSE

"Before I formed you in the womb I knew you,
before you were born I set you apart;
I appointed you as a prophet to the nations."

—JEREMIAH 1:5

I pray to cheerfully cheer others on, in Jesus' name, Amen.

DAY 2

IN THE WOMB...

This year has been a whirlwind of new experiences. I have a wider smile, and I am taller with my shoulders pulled back.

I earned a spot on the squad again, and I am elected captain. This is incredible! I can't believe it either. Pinch me!

I know the routines and can help my teammates like Lisa helped me, but am I ready? As the only remaining squad member, I have no choice but to step up and lead. I know I can do it, but for some reason I don't want to. It's easier to show up and follow others. *Why did I have to be the only one left?*

WALK DEEPER

1. Have you ever been a part of a team? What do you like the most? _____

    _____

    _____

2. How do you respond when you are asked to help others? _____

    _____

    _____

3. God knows you. What did HE put in you that others need? _____

    _____

    _____

MEMORY VERSE

"Before I formed you in the womb I knew you,
before you were born I set you apart;
I appointed you as a prophet to the nations."

—JEREMIAH 1:5

> *I pray to know you, God, like you know me, in Jesus' name, Amen.*

DAY 3

I KNEW YOU . . .

I don't feel ready or qualified, but it is up to me to teach, lead, and encourage twelve girls, including my baby sister who is the mascot.

Leadership as the cheer squad captain feels like herding cats. Have you ever tried to herd cats? If not, I will tell you: It is useless and exhausting. No one wants to listen. Everyone has ideas, yet they look to me for direction.

Gulp. *Why me?* I know I cannot do this.

Being a leader takes courage, discipline, and determination. While a great leader can bring great success, it also comes at the cost of being judged and overwhelmed. The Bible speaks of so many wonderful leaders and how God blessed them for their work. There are many verses and scriptures that God spoke to encourage men and women who choose to step up and lead.

> "Commit everything you do to the Lord.
> Trust him, and he will help you."
>
> —PSALM 37:5 (NLT)

"Wait patiently for the Lord. Be brave and courageous.
Yes, wait patiently for the Lord."

—PSALM 27:14 (NLT)

"Don't be afraid, for I am with you.
Don't be discouraged, for I am your God.
I will strengthen you and help you.
I will hold you up with my victorious right hand."

—ISAIAH 41:10 (NLT)

DEBORAH

There was a famous woman in the Bible named Deborah. She was a prophet and judge. Israelite judges were not like the judges we have today. A judge spoke for God and helped the Israelites defeat their enemies. Deborah gave judgments beneath a date palm tree!

Deborah was powerful because she was chosen by God to lead the people. Back in those times, women were not usually seen as leaders. But God used men *and* women. The Canaanites were their enemy, and they had been super mean to the Israelites for a long time. But God told Deborah to go to war with the Canaanites.

So Deborah told one of her leaders to gather an army to fight the Canaanite army in battle (Judges 4). Deborah was right there in the thick of the battle! She was brave because she knew God was on her side.

The Israelites defeated the enemy. Deborah does not question God's voice or wonder what others will say or think. She simply has the faith to do what God tells her. Whether people follow or not is not her concern. Her only desire is doing what the Lord has called her to, and not letting anything get in the way of that.

_____

I know I can cheer. God, help me know how to cheer and lead our squad well. I want everyone to have fun and do the best they know how.

WALK DEEPER

1. What does leadership mean to you? Share about your favorite leader. _____

   _____

   _____

2. Do you question what you are asked to do? What if it makes no sense?_____

   _____

   _____

3. When does God ask you to lead? _____

   _____

   _____

MEMORY VERSE

"Before I formed you in the womb I knew you,
before you were born I set you apart;
I appointed you as a prophet to the nations."

—JEREMIAH 1:5

> *I pray to lead like you do, God, in Jesus' name, Amen.*

DAY 4

BEFORE YOU WERE BORN...

I am running for student council eighth grade president. Against all boys. *What in the stars? A girl?* On top of that, I'm a girl no one knew until the year before. *Who do you think you are?*

Just like my Converse and tall socks, *I am doing it.* Mom shakes her head. I am a voice for the underdogs. The voiceless. Unfortunately, I lost by one vote. Bummer. I pretend not to care but cry in private. *What were you thinking? Why did you put yourself out there?*

Mom tried to warn me. Why didn't I listen? Everyone knows I lost. They are whispering again.

This time I give myself a pep rally. Great job for trying! I do my best to ignore the thoughts trying to push their way into my head.

Wait, you think you are so popular. You are still the shy, unknown, bullied girl hiding in the corner. Stop trying to earn approval and attention with your cool socks, shoes, and new glasses. Four eyes. I AM NOT.

I counter those thoughts with encouraging ones: *I cannot win or excel at everything. I am a winner no matter what.*

We have been through this already. Darn kids. School. Me. How many years of this is left? What will I do when I am on my own? Maybe others know something about me I do not know.

NOTE FROM GOD

Daughter, what would you do if I walked in the room? Right now. How would you praise and shout if I walked into the room? Right now. What would you say? Right now. I am with you. I know you. I am molding and preparing you (Isaiah 64:8). Continue to treat others how I treat you. I am here right now. You are a light like Deborah, even when you do not feel like it. I am your King, Savior, Provider, Healer, Redeemer, and Champion.

Just know I know you,

God

WALK DEEPER

1. What unfavorable memories play on repeat in your head? _____
    _____
    _____

2. How do you handle losing? Rejection? _____
    _____
    _____

3. Where is God before, during, and after a battle or situation? _____
    _____
    _____

MEMORY VERSE

"Before I formed you in the womb I knew you,
before you were born I set you apart;
I appointed you as a prophet to the nations."

—JEREMIAH 1:5

I pray to let go of disappointments quickly, in Jesus' name, Amen.

DAY 5

I SET YOU APART ...

I wish I could unknow what I now know about the dreaded "IT." Starts with the letter p and *flows*. I have been worried sick for three years. Everyone gets called up to the plate, and I am dead last in my class again.

My period makes a grand entrance, and I am caught off guard. It is nothing like I thought it would be. I might be dying. I do not say anything. This is weird—please stop. What if I am overreacting?

After two days of capital "F" for FEAR stamped across my forehead, Mom figures it out.

Maybe I should have learned sign language? We have been through the numbers and telling time rodeo. Now it is operating weird absorption tools. Stick with me.

It is summer and hot. I want to go swimming. Why on earth can't they have better instructions on the box? Yup, I am that girl. Somehow, I find the words and ask Mom for help. Scars me for life. Mom could care less, as she was an ER nurse. She has seen it all.

I eventually nailed it. I can't exactly "see" what I'm doing. I am flexible when I relax.

WALK DEEPER

1. Does the unknown scare you? What and why?_____
   _____
   _____

2. Are you able to ask for help easily or not? Share. _____
   _____
   _____

3. How is God helping you to be flexible and have more
   faith?_____
   _____
   _____

MEMORY VERSE

"Before I formed you in the womb I knew you,
before you were born I set you apart;
I appointed you as a prophet to the nations."

—JEREMIAH 1:5

*I pray to flow in your timing and not resist change,
in Jesus' name, Amen.*

DAY 6

I APPOINTED YOU...

Grandma Ruth knew somehow, even when I did not tell her. I am embarrassed she knows. My barely five foot, less-than-100-pound other grandma is the sweetest silver-haired lady who sits on two pillows to drive. She is practically a part of the steering wheel, perched up high to see the road.

I am sitting quietly in the passenger seat of her car when Grandma blurts out, "Did you get your period?"

Is there a sticker on my forehead? I must have leaked. Again. Surely my button bumps, boobies, did not give it away.

She sees my red face. "I never had a girl," she explains. "I raised three boys. I'm simply curious."

I am dying.

"Oh, how I hated cleaning my own rags when I was younger."

SAY WHAT? She must see the horror on my face.

"Well, you know in the olden days when I grew up, we didn't have luxury products like you have today."

Overwhelmed and confused, I am thankful for silence. I simply answer, "Yes, great, and I thought so."

The end.

WALK DEEPER

1. What do you know about your family lineage? Share.

   _____

   _____

   _____

2. How do their stories shift your perspective? _____

   _____

   _____

3. Who prays for you? What do you pray for future
   generations? _____

   _____

   _____

MEMORY VERSE

"Before I formed you in the womb I knew you,
before you were born I set you apart;
I appointed you as a prophet to the nations."

—JEREMIAH 1:5

> *I pray to carry and pass on my family mantle,*
> *in Jesus' name, Amen.*

DAY 7

AS A PROPHET TO THE NATIONS...

Middle school is wrapping up. Everyone is buzzing about where to attend high school. Our school is only kindergarten through eighth grade. I do not know which school is best, but I know I do not want to go to a large public school.

Times are tough. Mom and Dad work a lot. Their stress is obvious. Can I attend a private high school?

The private school is small, and most of my friends—alright *acquaintances*—will be attending. I beg. Okay, I whine. I persist until Mom and Dad come up with a proposal.

They say I must have skin in the game, but I know the real reason—there is not enough money. "We'll pay half the tuition. You pay the other half." Without hesitation or knowing how much, I shout, "Deal! I am in!"

Their plan backfired. They thought I would say no. Even my $1,000 portion per year did not deter me. "Where do I sign?"

I am a saver. I still have my pennies from first communion. I babysit, fold underwear, and sell lemonade out in the driveway. I will go door-to-door if I must. I know I got this.

I'm ALL IN.

WALK DEEPER

1. Do you like to save or spend? _____
    _____
    _____

2. Would you consider yourself an "ALL-IN" player? Explain.
    _____
    _____
    _____

3. What is God asking you to speak into existence? HINT:
    Say out loud what you want. _____
    _____
    _____

MEMORY VERSE

"Before I formed you in the womb I knew you,
before you were born I set you apart;
I appointed you as a prophet to the nations."

—JEREMIAH 1:5

I pray to always have childlike faith, in Jesus' name, Amen.

I KNOW YOU

PRAYER

Father, you know me. There is not a single thing about me hidden from your eyes. Encourage me to ask you first for help. Discipline me. Increase my determination. Help me to lead and show up like Deborah did. I want wisdom and faith like she had in you. The more I know you, the better I know me.

I love you,

Your ALL-IN known daughter

———————————————————————————————————

Sweet daughter, I do know you. All of you. I have known you. I will always outdo what you think you know. Just ask me.

Your forever loving daddy,

God

I KNOW YOU

DECLARATIONS FROM GOD

I know what inspires you.
I know your every thought.
I know your heart's desire.
I know your strengths and weaknesses.
I know you are brave.
I know what is in you.
I know you are determined.
I know what you need.
I know I delight in you.
I know how to stretch you.
I know I will never leave you.
I know how to love you.
I know what fills you up.
I know you inside and out.

WEEK 5

JUST BE

MEMORY VERSE

"Be still, and know that I *am* God;
I will be exalted among the nations,
I will be exalted in the earth!"

—PSALM 46:10 (NKJV)

DAY 1

BE STILL . . .

I am shaking like a leaf, but I am ready. It doesn't feel real, but the first day of high school is here. *This must be a dream.*

I am sporting my new uniform, grey lace-up shoes, knee-high socks, and backpack as I enter a huge building among hundreds of unfamiliar faces. I have already endured a school bus transfer, and now I need to figure out important things like who I will sit with in class and how in the world I will find my classrooms.

Let us not discuss opening the locker, which floor, what homeroom, and the thought of eating alone in the cafeteria. Excruciating. I am gripped with fear yet calm, as I am used to paving the way for my younger siblings and cousins. Even so, I feel like shouting, "Why do I always have to go first?!"

False **E**vidence **A**ppearing **R**eal

FEAR IS A BULLY.

WALK DEEPER

1. Do you like to be first or last? Why? _____
    _____
    _____

2. Are you able to be still? How? _____
    _____
    _____

3. God is not a bully. Who is a bully, and why?_____
    _____
    _____

MEMORY VERSE

"Be still, and know that I *am* God;
I will be exalted among the nations,
I will be exalted in the earth!"

—PSALM 46:10 (NKJV)

I pray for your equipping peace, in Jesus' name, Amen.

DAY 2

I earned a spot on the freshman cheerleading squad, and I am excited to meet new teammates and make friends. The awkwardness is starting to disappear. I am settling into a routine.

I am nominated and elected the freshman football homecoming attendant. I am shocked, but thrilled! Our class voted, and I received the most votes. *Did they count correctly*?

They do not know me. I'm the girl everyone used to pick on and wanted to avoid. Remember the mean girls in the bathroom, the kickball rejection, and counting on my fingers. I am still wearing tie shoes and might slap you, so beware. Impostor. Maybe high school is different? I am still guarding my heart in case. That way, rejection will not sting as much. I hope.

WALK DEEPER

1. Do you love yourself? How?_____

    _____

    _____

2. Are you able to receive love from others?_____

    _____

    _____

3. How does God know your heart? _____

    _____

    _____

MEMORY VERSE

"Be still, and know that I *am* God;
I will be exalted among the nations,
I will be exalted in the earth!"

—PSALM 46:10 (NKJV)

I pray to just be loved by you, in Jesus' name, Amen.

DAY 3

THAT I AM GOD . . .

No one knows I use myself as a punching bag to toughen me up. Have you ever done this? I am hard on myself. The battle in my head is real.

I am determined and only *appear* to have it together. I work harder than most but am a slave to everything around me. No wonder no one knows the real me. How can they if I cannot be the real me?

Surrendering is not an option. I cannot be weak. That is how I get hurt. So I think. The speed bag beats the lesson into me. If I do not say or do the wrong thing, then people will accept me.

What a lie.

I feel like Ebenezer Scrooge. The script turned. I am nice, gentle, and forgiving with everyone around me—except myself. I am miserable on the inside, but no one knows. I hide it well.

My heart is hardening. I pretend to be soft. I want it to stop.

WALK DEEPER

1. When do you pretend to be someone else? Explain.

    _____

    _____

    _____

2. Do you act the same in private and in public?_____

    _____

    _____

3. How does God want you to be? _____

    _____

    _____

MEMORY VERSE

"Be still, and know that I *am* God;
I will be exalted among the nations,
I will be exalted in the earth!"

—PSALM 46:10 (NKJV)

I pray to be the real and authentic me, in Jesus' name, Amen.

DAY 4

I WILL BE EXALTED...

I have a crush on a senior. Our families are friends. Flirting is fun. So is being noticed by a boy. One night while I'm studying, the phone rings. I am in shock. He calls and asks me to attend the homecoming dance with him!

Me?!

I plan to attend with a group of single classmates, both guys and girls, since I do not have a boyfriend. This will make it even better. *Yes, I will go*!

Wouldn't you?

I run downstairs, breathless with excitement, shouting, "I have a date for homecoming!"

All goes silent.

"What? With who?!!"

"He's a senior. You are a freshman. You are *not* going with him."

"We're friends and know his family."

"We don't care—it looks bad."

"Looks bad? To who?"

"Everyone, that's who."

I am baffled by the "everyone and what will people think" response. Do other people really care?

"You're not calling him back. Girls do not call boys. Tell him at school you are sorry. You didn't check with your parents first and are not able to go with him."

I am Mortified with a capital "M." I did not want to hurt his feelings. "He is nice to me," I plead.

It is a NO.

WALK DEEPER

1. Share a time you were completely shocked. How did you feel? _____

    _____

    _____

2. Do you struggle with pleasing people? HINT: Making others happy even when you're not? Explain. _____

    _____

    _____

3. How do you please God more than man?_____

    _____

    _____

MEMORY VERSE

"Be still, and know that I *am* God;
I will be exalted among the nations,
I will be exalted in the earth!"

—PSALM 46:10 (NKJV)

> *I pray to desire only what you think, not others, God,
> in Jesus' name, Amen.*

DAY 5

AMONG THE NATIONS...

feel terrible telling him yes then no to homecoming. I know I should have asked first, but disappointment stinks. Rejection stings. We are human. Unfortunately, we hurt people even when we do not mean to.

I secretly make another declaration: *If I commit to someone or something, I will not let them down.* I can be trusted.

I have learned to speak up, ask good questions, and wait. I give myself permission to say no, even though I know the other person may cringe and feel defeated when they hear it. Saying yes to everything is not good.

ADAM AND EVE

The first book of the Bible is Genesis. In the beginning, Adam and Eve were incredibly happy. They lived a beautiful life in the Garden of Eden. They had animals to talk to and various trees to eat fruits from. God allowed them to eat fruits from every tree in the garden, except for the Tree of the Knowledge of Good and Evil.

While walking along the center of the garden, there was beautiful fruit hanging on the forbidden tree. Eve was deceived and believed the serpent's lies that it was okay to eat. She took a bite.

As the fruit was delicious, she insisted Adam take a bite too. He did. Adam disobeyed God's command (Romans 5:12–21). For the first time, Adam and Eve realized they were naked and covered their bodies with leaves.

God knew of their wrong deed and was angry. Adam blamed Eve and told God he ate the fruit on Eve's insistence. She blamed it on the serpent. Sadly, they blamed each other. God punished Adam and Eve by banishing them from the Garden of Eden and said that they would have to live a hard life outside of paradise.

Life is about choices. We choose to say yes or no. Eve's lesson was costly. God can be trusted but Satan cannot. Whenever we choose our selfish desires over those of God, bad consequences will follow.

WALK DEEPER

1. How do you handle disappointment? _____

   _____

   _____

2. Have you ever made a choice you regretted? _____

   _____

   _____

3. Do you ask God before you decide? Share. _____

   _____

   _____

MEMORY VERSE

"Be still, and know that I *am* God;
I will be exalted among the nations,
I will be exalted in the earth!"

—PSALM 46:10 (NKJV)

> *I pray to obey you only, God, in Jesus' name, Amen.*

DAY 6

I WILL BE EXALTED . . .

I am not a part of the social scene. Not invited. I overhear others talking in the halls and in class. They chat excitedly about weekend gatherings, sleepovers, and movies.

I am not in the "popular" group because I do not party. I admit I am a goody-two-shoes. Not a bad thing. Regardless, I am nice to everyone.

I am not allowed to ride home with a friend if a meeting or practice is canceled or ends early. I only hope I remember a quarter to call home if I forget something I need for school. Otherwise, I'll hear about it from Mom. Payphones, practice, homework, and classmates. So much to juggle.

I do not want to disappoint my parents, myself, or my siblings. I am the oldest at home, but youngest in class. I'm rigid at times, so fearful of making a mistake that I follow all the rules and freeze when I'm not sure what the "right" thing is to do. Am I a forty-year-old trapped in a teenage body? I just need to be me—comfortable in my own skin.

NOTE FROM GOD

Breathe and take one step at a time. You are not alone. You can do this. You will make it! Be still and know that I am God! (Psalm 46:10). Trust the process. You are beginning a new adventure that will have curves, turns, ups and downs. It is not what you see; it is what you do not.

Just be you,

God

WALK DEEPER

1. Are you a rule follower or rule breaker? Why or why not?

   _____
   _____
   _____

2. How do you feel when you disappoint yourself or others? _____

   _____
   _____

3. Are you relaxed with God and able to just be you? Share.

   _____
   _____
   _____

MEMORY VERSE

"Be still, and know that I *am* God;
I will be exalted among the nations,
I will be exalted in the earth!"

—PSALM 46:10 (NKJV)

> *I pray to not compromise what I know is right,*
> *in Jesus' name, Amen.*

DAY 7

IN THE EARTH...

I am asked to play fastpitch softball as a guest for another team—ballpark lights on and fields packed, with players twice my size and intimidating. I strike out and never touch the ball on the field. After the game, the coach asks if I want to join their team.

I am not interested. "Thanks for the chance, but this is not for me."

"Can't you at least try? If you keep your eye on the ball, despite your misses, you will eventually connect."

"Nope, I'm out."

I walk away defeated, quitting before I give it a chance. Honestly, I am afraid. A year later, I try out for the high school fastpitch team. I feel comfortable, even though I know some of the girls are better than me.

On the same day, I try out for Wizard of Oz and get the role of Glinda! I am thinking I can do both fastpitch and the play since I will only have two lines. It will be fun!

I am blindsided when my coach pulls me into the office, saying I must decide between one or the other before the roster is determined. I cannot do both.

I choose the safe, guaranteed route, playing Glinda. I convince myself I am not good enough to make the team. I am wrong.

"You would have made the team," Coach tells me the next day. "You *can* play. I wanted you to decide. It's too late now."

It's a heavy consequence for my lack of confidence. I can play. I just need to step up to the plate.

WALK DEEPER

1. What are some valuable lessons you have learned choosing the comfortable route? _____

    _____

    _____

2. Are you able to keep your eyes on the ball? Explain. ____

    _____

    _____

3. How does God help you make wise decisions?_____

    _____

    _____

MEMORY VERSE

"Be still, and know that I am God;
I will be exalted among the nations,
I will be exalted in the earth!"

—PSALM 46:10 (NKJV)

I pray for an increase in confidence, in Jesus' name, Amen.

JUST BE

PRAYER

Father, thank you for continuing to help me remove the logs from my own eyes (Matthew 7:3). Thank you for showing me how to be and making me just the way I am. Thank you that I get to be me. Forgive me for the times I've beaten myself up. I do forgive myself, with your help. Forgive me for disobeying when I know better. Thank you for increasing my faith. Thank you. I have a safe place to be me. I am grateful for your daily mercy and grace.

Your humble daughter

Sweet daughter, be you. Just be who I designed you to be. Do not fear. Ever. You will experience me even more.

Your forever loving daddy,

God

JUST BE

DECLARATIONS FROM GOD

Just be you.
Just be still.
Just be fearless.
Just be flexible.
Just be present.
Just be thankful.
Just be surrendered.
Just be real.
Just be honest.
Just be diligent.
Just be at peace.
Just be content.
Just be expectant.
Just be free.

WEEK 6

LET ME

MEMORY VERSE

"Jesus answered, 'I am the way and the truth and the life. No one comes to the Father except through me.'"

—JOHN 14:6

DAY 1

JESUS ANSWERED...

A new classmate creates a buzz. He is a heartthrob from our rival high school. There is whispering in the halls and suddenly attention turns my way. I look behind me. Oh shoot, no one's there.

Who are you looking at? Wait. *ME?!* Am I dreaming again? Hold on. Flutters in my stomach rush heat to my cheeks and leave me momentarily incapable of breathing. I cannot believe this is happening, but somehow this boy that everyone is crushing on has chosen me.

Awkward flirting and phone conversations begin. I am not even sure what we are talking about. I listen. I can barely concentrate or breathe. I'm thinking there are so many pretty girls with money, designer shoes, clothes, and purses. *He chooses me.* I don't understand why.

WALK DEEPER

1. Are you aware of what is going on around you? Share.

    _____

    _____

    _____

2. What does flirt mean to you? _____

    _____

    _____

3. God chooses you. Will you let Him? _____

    _____

    _____

MEMORY VERSE

"Jesus answered, 'I am the way and the truth and the life. No
one comes to the Father except through me.'"

—JOHN 14:6

> *I pray I always choose you first, God, in Jesus' name, Amen.*

DAY 2

I AM THE WAY...

My middle name is *naive*. I have had two kisses on the cheek until now, not counting my dad.

My two-week boyfriend just wants to make out. *Gross.* I am content with holding hands.

After football games, his hands attempt to touch places. I quickly move them while trying to figure out if I am kissing right. Ugh.

What is happening? This is not okay. Things are moving too fast, and I am not feeling right about it. I never understood the birds and the bees talk in middle school. Awkward. I acted like I knew but did not have a clue. Probably should have paid better attention.

How do I balance wanting to be liked, fitting in, and not doing something wrong? I wish I dared to ask questions without feeling dumb.

WALK DEEPER

1. Do you feel awkward around boys? Explain. _____
    _____
    _____

2. Have you been in a position you did not know what to
    do?_____
    _____
    _____

3. What questions do you ask God? What does HE ask you?
    _____
    _____
    _____

MEMORY VERSE

"Jesus answered, 'I am the way and the truth and the life. No
one comes to the Father except through me.'"

—JOHN 14:6

I pray for courage and understanding, in Jesus' name, Amen.

DAY 3

AND THE TRUTH…

We are talking while walking in the hall between classes, and my mind begins to race along with my heart. *Did he just say what I think he said?*

"Hey, I think it's time we're just friends."

Palms sweaty and face flushed, I'm silent with shock but try not to let on that I'm upset.

"You're nice, but I like someone else. Are you okay?"

I am fighting back tears and searching for a response.

"I am sorry. I hope you understand."

I can barely catch my breath or think straight. I manage to say without skipping a beat, "I agree, and I'm completely fine."

"Oh, fantastic—I was worried you would be upset. See you around."

And off he went. Just like that. Door slammed.

WALK DEEPER

1. When have you had to hold your tears back? Share. ____
   _____
   _____

2. Do you stuff, ignore, or confront your pain? How? _____
   _____
   _____

3. Where is God when others leave you behind? Share. ___
   _____
   _____

MEMORY VERSE

"Jesus answered, 'I am the way and the truth and the life.
No one comes to the Father except through me.'"

—JOHN 14:6

I pray to speak truth and respond with love, in Jesus' name, Amen.

DAY 4

AND THE LIFE...

W hispering continues. The whole school knows. "I didn't think it was my place to say anything," my friend says.

In my head I'm thinking, *Are you kidding? What kind of friend are you?* "What do you mean?" I ask.

"There were parties over break," says my friend. "Boys, girls, and cheerleading teammates." She's clearly uncomfortable sharing, but I know she knows.

"Is another cheerleader dating him?"

"Yes," she replies.

"When I thought I was?"

"Yes."

"She was *with* him."

Let that sink in. My head is spinning, not sure what to think. I would not let him touch me, but she had no problem with it. I thought she was a friend, and he was my boyfriend. I clearly do not understand relationships. Let us not talk about morals, cheating, or doing the right thing. What is wrong with people? I am stunned, but I'm glad I didn't let him touch me or do things I'm not ready for.

WALK DEEPER

1. Has a friend ever turned their back on you? Did you know why?_____

    _____

    _____

2. How do you feel when others know something you do not?_____

    _____

    _____

3. When hurtful truth is revealed, where is God? _____

    _____

    _____

MEMORY VERSE

"Jesus answered, 'I am the way and the truth and the life. No one comes to the Father except through me.'"

—JOHN 14:6

I pray to be honest and pure, in Jesus' name, Amen.

DAY 5

NO ONE COMES...

Betrayal. Someone you trust lies, cheats, or hurts you, putting themself first. I looked it up in the dictionary. This happened to me. Boyfriend gone.

I am not quitting cheerleading because my teammate took my boyfriend. Neither is she, but maybe he told her we already broke up or we were just friends and the joke's on me. I thought we were more than friends. I don't kiss just anyone. Who knows? I cannot find words to say or thoughts to think. The pain is unbearable.

I don't even know where to begin. I act as though nothing happened. So do they. I avoid him and ignore my teammate. They do the same. It does not seem right. No one cares.

I am not sure why we cannot have an honest discussion face-to-face. Instead, we avoid each other and brush it all under the rug. What's done is done. I will gather myself and move on.

WALK DEEPER

1. Have you been betrayed? Betrayed someone else? _____

    _____

    _____

2. How do you process pain? _____

    _____

    _____

3. Do you put God first? Does HE put you first? Explain. ___

    _____

    _____

MEMORY VERSE

"Jesus answered, 'I am the way and the truth and the life.
No one comes to the Father except through me.'"

—JOHN 14:6

I pray to learn from painful experiences, in Jesus' name, Amen.

DAY 6

TO THE FATHER...

My heart aches, and the wind blows out of my spirit. I have the hardest time letting things go, especially when someone hurts me. Forgiveness is last on my list. All I can hear in my head is, "You're a nice girl. I never wanted to hurt you." Too late. You did.

How can friends hurt one another without thinking twice? After all the backstabbing and ignoring, I just get more fake apologies and lying. What happened to treating others as you want to be treated?

I do not need boys. They are stupid.

PETER

In the Bible, Peter lies about knowing Jesus. Jesus had been arrested. Peter was scared. A servant girl asked Peter if he was one of Jesus' friends. Peter lied. "I don't know what you are talking about," he said. (I have been there!) The servant girl told some other people that she thought Peter was one of Jesus' friends. Peter got angry and said, "I don't know Him!" Later, some other people said, "You must be one of Jesus' friends."

Peter was still afraid and said, "I don't know the man!" Right away, a rooster began to crow. Peter remembered Jesus' words, that Peter would lie about Him three times before a rooster crowed in the morning. Peter went outside and cried. Later, Jesus showed He still loved Peter. He forgave Peter.

Despite our human weaknesses, failures, and sins, Jesus is eager to forgive us and restore our relationship with Him. He commands us to do the same. You can find this story in the following verses: Matthew 26:69–75; Mark 14:66–72; Luke 22:55–62; John 18:15–18, 25–27.

WALK DEEPER

1. Do you forgive easily? Share._____
    _____
    _____

2. Have you denied someone you love, like Peter did?_____
    _____
    _____

3. How does God restore broken relationships?_____
    _____
    _____

MEMORY VERSE

"Jesus answered, 'I am the way and the truth and the life.
No one comes to the Father except through me.'"

—JOHN 14:6

Help me to forgive others as you forgive me, in Jesus' name, Amen.

DAY 7
EXCEPT THROUGH ME . . .

Hurt people hurt people. I am guilty too. It's junior year, and I have gone on a few dates. Always as friends. My heart is not open for business. I am guarded and reinforced with heavy artillery. I do not want to be hurt again.

A boy in class likes me, and I pretend to reciprocate. We have been good friends the last few years. I enjoy his friendship. He is nice and fun to hang out with, but I feel like he wants to date seriously. I do not want to hurt him. I write a letter. Why do I feel just as bad being "the crusher"? He walks away.

This relationship thing is complicated. The sting lasts.

WALK DEEPER

1. Is your heart open or closed? Soft or hard? Explain. ___
    _____
    _____

2. Have you ever had to let a friend go? Share. _____
    _____
    _____

3. How can you let God direct your steps?_____
    _____
    _____

MEMORY VERSE

Jesus answered, "I am the way and the truth and the life.
No one comes to the Father except through me."

—JOHN 14:6

> *I pray for a deep relationship with you, God, in Jesus' name, Amen.*

LET ME

PRAYER

Jesus, we thank you for forgiving Peter when he said he did not know you, and we thank you for forgiving us of our sins too. Help me to forgive quickly like you forgive me. Help me to love you my whole life and to teach other people about you. Keep my heart soft and open.

Help me not to hurt you or others,

Your tender daughter

Sweet daughter, let me in your heart. Let me love you.

Forgiveness doesn't excuse their behavior. Forgiveness prevents their behavior from destroying your heart.

Forgive them like I forgive you (Ephesians 4:32).

Your forever loving daddy,

God

LET ME

DECLARATIONS FROM GOD

Let me captivate you.
Let me in.
Let me show you what I have just for you.
Let me lead the way.
Let me direct your steps.
Let me help you.
Let me be your best friend.
Let me teach you.
Let me hold you.
Let me run with you.
Let me bless you.
Let me renew you.
Let me write your story.
Let me surround you.

WEEK 7

I AM RIGHT HERE

MEMORY VERSE

"For I am the LORD your God, who upholds your right hand,
Who says to you, 'Do not fear, I will help you.'"

—ISAIAH 41:13 (NASB)

DAY 1

FOR I AM...

Our underdog division III Ohio football team wins state! Stadiums are packed, rain or shine. The school and community are ecstatic. I love being on the sidelines cheering the team on to victory.

I understand why surrounding competitors are so passionate about winning. It feels amazing! Several local powerhouse teams experience nonstop victories. Not us. We have been laughed at and overlooked. We are a small private school. Now that we got a taste of it, we want more.

This unexpected success is brand new. *Is this a dream*? Wait, this is happening, and we are the winners. All things are possible.

WALK DEEPER

1. Have you been a part of a winning team or on the
   sidelines? Share. _____
   _____
   _____

2. How do you handle success? Positive attention?_____
   _____
   _____

3. Do you give credit to God? How?_____
   _____
   _____

MEMORY VERSE

"For I am the LORD your God, who upholds your right hand,
Who says to you, 'Do not fear, I will help you.'"

—ISAIAH 41:13 (NASB)

I believe nothing is impossible with you, God, in Jesus' name, Amen.

DAY 2
THE LORD YOUR GOD...

It is opening night for our annual spring school play, *The Wizard of Oz.* The excitement is contagious, as we have been rehearsing for weeks. Lines are memorized, costumes designed, and props created. Volunteers have worked tirelessly to transform our school gymnasium.

I play Glinda, who looks out for Dorothy. I have two lines I know forwards and backwards. Even though I was scared of my own shadow in elementary school and couldn't speak up for myself, I love being on stage now.

Though I once struggled to understand how people could perform without missing a beat—making it look effortless, fun, and free—I know now how actors, singers, and dancers make their talent look easy. Talent is in them, just like you and me. "Dorothy, you had the power all along, my dear," says Glinda. Your role matters.

WALK DEEPER

1. What power or talents do you have?_____
    _____
    _____

2. What things are hard for you? _____
    _____
    _____

3. Why does God give different gifts? Share._____
    _____
    _____

MEMORY VERSE

"For I am the LORD your God, who upholds your right hand,
Who says to you, 'Do not fear, I will help you.'"

—ISAIAH 41:13 (NASB)

> *I pray you pull out the talent in me, God, in Jesus' name, Amen.*

DAY 3

WHO UPHOLDS . . .

I am here to experience it all, so I decided to run track. Truthfully, it's more to stay in shape and prepare for upcoming cheerleading tryouts. Mom shakes her head but thinks it is a good idea. I don't really like running, but I know consistent training will help build my strength.

Track practice is much harder than I anticipated. I like being pushed in practice but cannot stand the meets. Competitors run circles around me. I finish last and hate that I am the SLOWEST. I am five-foot-nothing and can walk faster backward.

I ask the coach if I can just attend practices, so I do not hold the team back. I just want to skip the meets and focus on training. He scratches his head, looks at me funny, but agrees. "Trust me, this will put both of us out of our misery," I say.

I own the "track practice" role. I do not have a school record, medal, or participation award. I do have 100 percent attendance. For six weeks. Mom always says, "Finish what you start and follow through no matter what." I victoriously completed six weeks of practice. Ready to try out!

WALK DEEPER

1. Do you feel stretched when you try new things? Share.

   _____
   _____
   _____

2. Do you finish what you start? Explain. _____

   _____
   _____

3. How does God help you run your race?_____

   _____
   _____

MEMORY VERSE

"For I am the LORD your God, who upholds your right hand,
Who says to you, 'Do not fear, I will help you.'"

—ISAIAH 41:13 (NASB)

> *I pray you help me, God, when I get off track, in Jesus' name, Amen.*

A NOTE FROM GOD

"Don't you realize that in a race everyone runs, but only one person gets the prize? So run to win! All athletes are disciplined in their training. They do it to win a prize that will fade away, but we do it for an eternal prize. So I run with purpose in every step. I am not just shadowboxing."

—*1 Corinthians 9:24–26, NLT*

DAY 4

I bumped up my "nerd" status by joining TI, Teenage Institute—teens who agree not to drink, drink and drive, or take drugs. I do not care if friends snicker. You already do anyway.

I am not invited to many private social gatherings. I am a goody-two-shoes. TI gives me the automatic "out," and I think it is a good group. I am not missing out. I've chosen right.

MARY AND MARTHA

"Jesus is coming! Jesus is coming!" Mary shouted to her sister Martha as she came running into the house (Luke 10:38–42). Mary and Martha shared the work of keeping their home clean. But now Mary was so happy she could hardly wait. It had been a long time since she had seen Jesus.

Jesus and His disciples arrived. Mary and Martha went to the door to welcome Him. Mary was so interested she stopped her work when Jesus came. She sat close and listened to Jesus so she would not miss a single word He said. Jesus told many wonderful stories.

While Mary was listening to Jesus, Martha was worrying about getting dinner ready. She wanted everything to be "just right." Martha got tired of doing all the work by herself. She complained to Jesus, "Lord, it isn't fair that I am doing all the work while Mary just sits there. Tell her to come and help me."

Jesus answered, "Martha, Martha, you worry about too many things. What Mary is hearing is more important than serving or eating. She has chosen the right thing, and it will not be taken away from her."

Wow! Jesus spoke up for Mary, even though Martha thought she was being lazy. But Mary knew what was important—spending time with Jesus and listening to His teaching. She knew it was a special opportunity to be near Jesus, and she did not want to miss anything!

———————

I confess to worrying about what others think of me and not pausing what I am doing to pay attention. I have to remind myself to be still. I don't want to miss anything you have for me, God. Help me hear what you are saying.

WALK DEEPER

1. When do you worry? Share why or why not. _____
    _____
    _____

2. Do you get distracted with busyness? Are you a good
    listener? _____
    _____
    _____

3. How do you give God your full attention? _____
    _____
    _____

MEMORY VERSE

"For I am the LORD your God, who upholds your right hand,
Who says to you, 'Do not fear, I will help you.'"

—ISAIAH 41:13 (NASB)

> *I pray to not miss what you are saying to me, God,*
> *in Jesus' name, Amen.*

DAY 5
WHO SAYS TO YOU...

It is a rainy, dreary day, so cheerleading practice is inside in the dim, chilly, rundown gym that echoes. It feels depressing with empty stands and folded-up hoops.

We stretch and begin practicing one of our routines. As quickly as the pyramid goes up, it crumbles back down even faster in a tidal wave of bodies—nothing we experienced before.

I am standing on my teammate's shoulders. She freezes as we watch everyone fall around us in slow motion. Instead of reaching for my hands, she grips my calves even tighter. I am doing my best to balance but have nothing to hold onto. My arms begin to flail, causing me to fall face forward on the gym floor. Everyone gasps.

Time stands still. I cannot think, feel, or make sense of the situation. We help one another stand up, inspecting for injuries. I am the only one. Half of my front tooth is missing. My teammates' faces say it all.

Calls are frantically made. My tooth is found across the floor and now floats in a cup of cold water. I can feel the pain, but I do not want to see it. I want to panic but remain calm. My self-conscious head is spinning.

WALK DEEPER

1. Have you experienced an unexpected accident? Share.

   _____

   _____

   _____

2. How do you feel when you are not in control? _____

   _____

   _____

3. Where is God when things are falling apart? _____

   _____

   _____

MEMORY VERSE

"For I am the LORD your God, who upholds your right hand,
Who says to you, 'Do not fear, I will help you.'"

—ISAIAH 41:13 (NASB)

> *I pray to remain calm despite what life looks like,*
> *in Jesus' name, Amen.*

DAY 6
DO NOT FEAR...

Why me? I have my bald spot, four eyes, space between front teeth, two left feet, lack of clothing or makeup ability, hairy legs, and now I have a half front tooth to attempt to fit in?

Timing is everything. Did this have to happen today? Tonight kicks off our annual local summer rib cook-off and festival. All my friends will be there. Never mind the excruciating pain. I am in shock, yet relaxed. I feel numb.

My parents are working, so Grandpa and Grandma race to the rescue, picking up my brother and me in front of the school. He was practicing with the soccer team when told, "Come quick. Your sister is fine, but she had an accident. Your family is on the way to pick you both up." Truthfully, I want Mom and Dad.

He came running around the school building, hugged me, and said, "I am right here. All is going to be fine." My family's faces painted the same picture of concern.

I said goodbye to my teammates without a tear, gripping my iced water cup containing my bobbing tooth. This is not exactly how I thought this day would turn out. We headed across town to the dentist in silence. I could not help but think about this ironic curveball. There are no coincidences. I know in my heart my broken tooth is no exception.

I always smile, but with my mouth closed. I despise the large space between my two front buck teeth. A semi could fit between them. I am not joking. I confess I tie dental floss around my old "Buckies" at night, hoping for beautifully aligned front teeth in the morning. It has never happened. Now one is broken in half.

WALK DEEPER

1. Do you like curveballs? How do you handle them? _____
   _____
   _____

2. Do you find yourself asking, "Why me?" when something
   bad happens? Explain. _____
   _____
   _____

3. How do you lean on God during trials? _____
   _____
   _____

MEMORY VERSE

"For I am the LORD your God, who upholds your right hand,
Who says to you, 'Do not fear, I will help you.'"

—ISAIAH 41:13 (NASB)

I pray to trust you and know you have me, in Jesus' name, Amen.

DAY 7

I WILL HELP YOU…

The dentist chair is hard and uncomfortable. The office is sterile and smells like medicine. I am not sure the soft background music is soothing. I do not like it here yet, do I? My dream of beautifully aligned front teeth with a sign of "no travel zone here" may be coming true.

Sixteen shots of Novocain later, multiple root canals, pain medication, ice, liquids, and I am back together like Mrs. Potato Head.

My brand new "bonded" front teeth are beautiful! No space?! I keep checking. Still together.

Within two weeks, my new bonded white front straight-together non-bucking teeth are beautiful. Pinch me! I cannot stop smiling ear to ear with my mouth open. I will never be the same. My before and after pictures say it all. I will never forget this. Ever.

WALK DEEPER

1. What do you like about your smile? _____

    _____

    _____

2. How do you feel when something ends up better than it
    started? _____

    _____

    _____

3. When God shows up unexpectedly, how do you
    respond? Share. _____

    _____

    _____

MEMORY VERSE

"For I am the LORD your God, who upholds your right hand,
Who says to you, 'Do not fear, I will help you.'"

—ISAIAH 41:13 (NASB)

> *I pray to always give you thanks, in Jesus' name, Amen.*

I AM RIGHT HERE

PRAYER

Thank you, Jesus, for always being with me and for filling me with your power. Thank you for celebrating and protecting me, always holding my hand. Thank you for sitting with me, even in the dentist's chair. Healing my bruises. Reminding me not to worry. Help me focus on you. Please whisper in my ear and remind me who I am. I know you will never leave me. You always show up and show off. Thank you for answering my prayers.

I love you,

Your obedient daughter

_____

Sweet daughter, I am right here. I love you. I am right here holding your hand.

Your forever loving daddy,

God

I AM RIGHT HERE

DECLARATIONS FROM GOD

I am right here next to you.
I am right here holding you.
I am right here looking at you.
I am right here wiping your tears.
I am right here answering your questions.
I am right here helping you.
I am right here protecting you.
I am right here waiting for you.
I am right here cheering you on.
I am right here cautioning you.
I am right here preparing you.
I am right here pursuing you.
I am right here adoring you.
I am right here blessing you.

WEEK 8

LET GO

MEMORY VERSE

"Pour out all your worries and stress upon him *and leave them there*, for he always tenderly cares for you."

—1 PETER 5:7 (TPT)

DAY 1

POUR OUT . . .

I have been riding the yellow school bus for eleven years and counting. I am an expert after countless hours bouncing up and down.

I like to sit by myself in the middle. Right side. Window down and not on the "hump"—you know, the giant mound that forces your knees to your chest. The hump makes it hard to sit, let alone breathe. I must pay attention and choose wisely.

No seat belts are a mystery. Apparently only the driver needs this safety feature.

I enjoyed climbing aboard my first eight years. It was a fun adventure to and from school! Around the time I transitioned to high school, riding the bus had long lost its luster.

My friends quickly disappear from the seats around me. Most are riding with friends who are driving, older siblings, neighbors, or they are simply turning sixteen and driving themselves. Some proudly announce their bus riding retirement, while others vanish without a word. It makes me sad. I hope someday I can ride with a friend, with no stops and less time wasted. For now, I am still on the bus as an upperclassman, and this is embarrassing. I want to let go of this transportation option. It may not seem like a big deal, but it is to me. I know there is more freedom. I want it.

WALK DEEPER

1. What is your favorite type of transportation? Why? _____
   _____
   _____

2. How do you respond when others have choices, and
   you do not? Share. _____
   _____
   _____

3. How does God pour His love out on you? _____
   _____
   _____

MEMORY VERSE

"Pour out all your worries and stress upon him *and leave them
there*, for he always tenderly cares for you."

—1 PETER 5:7 (TPT)

> *I pray to appreciate adventures with you, God,
> in Jesus' name, Amen.*

DAY 2

I dream about turning sixteen. I can feel the freedom—the day I can drive or ride with a friend straight to school and back instead of fifty-two stops. Yes, I am exaggerating.

Pursuing alternate transportation is not an option with Mom. She says, "The bus is the safest option. I do not need another thing to worry about, plus you and your brother are together. That makes me feel better."

I have friends who offer rides. "Thank you for thinking of me. My parents said I'm not allowed."

I beg. "Can I please ride with my friend?" The answer remains.

"Stop asking. This is not up for discussion," Mom says.

Denied for now.

A NOTE FROM GOD

Let go to make space for all the new things I have for you.

It is a choice to remove your worry (Proverbs 12:25). Let go of your old patterns, habits, and limiting beliefs. It is time to move forward with me. Letting go is a healthy way to maintain joy and peace in your heart.

WALK DEEPER

1. What do you dream about? _____
   _____
   _____

2. What does freedom mean to you? Explain. _____
   _____
   _____

3. Do you beg or ask God for things? Share. _____
   _____
   _____

MEMORY VERSE

"Pour out all your worries and stress upon him *and leave them
there*, for he always tenderly cares for you."

—1 PETER 5:7 (TPT)

> *I pray I never stop asking you questions, God, in Jesus' name, Amen.*

DAY 3

AND STRESS . . .

"Why?" That three-letter word gets me in trouble. I do not like hearing "because I said so." That does not answer my questions. I persist.

"Riding with inexperienced teenage drivers is dangerous. I do not trust them, and accidents happen fast. I worked in the emergency room and have seen it all," Mom says.

Fair enough. I agree safety is important. Mom and Dad care.

Still, I beg. No budging. Offer up everything I own.

Still, I hear "no," which means "not right now" to me.

HANNAH

In the Bible, Hannah (1 Samuel 1:2–2:21) is an example of perseverance in prayer. She prayed nonstop for a child until God granted her request. Hannah did not give up asking! She had faith the Lord would hear her and answer her prayers.

Hannah vowed to give her son to the Lord. When Samuel was born, she allowed him to be raised in the temple as promised. Samuel eventually became the last of Israel's judges, a prophet, and a counselor to Kings Saul and David.

Hannah's story teaches us that asking for a miracle at God's hand is not always wrong. Hannah accepted God's promise with unwavering faith. God answered her prayers, and Hannah fulfilled her promise. She was willing to give everything to the Lord.

Do not ever give up praying and asking. There is a difference between persistence in something good like Hannah and persistence because of stubbornness. Wisdom separates the two.

I sound ungrateful, but I am thankful. I will continue to ride and not complain. I have learned this only makes things worse. I am waiting—expectantly.

WALK DEEPER

1. Do you ask "why" a lot? _____

    _____

    _____

2. When are you persistent? Share._____

    _____

    _____

3. How does God bless you when you put HIM first and
    wait for HIS answer? Explain. _____

    _____

    _____

MEMORY VERSE

"Pour out all your worries and stress upon him *and leave them
there*, for he always tenderly cares for you."

—1 PETER 5:7 (TPT)

I pray I faithfully trust your timing, God, in Jesus' name, Amen.

DAY 4

UPON HIM . . .

Verbally asking has not worked. Not one time. I resort to a handwritten letter baring my mind, heart, and soul, entitled "Old Yeller, My School Bus Break Up." I plead my case once again and beg not to be the only senior riding the bus. Just a chance. It is my last shot to voice my case.

The letter bypasses Mom and lands on Dad's dresser right where he can see. I hate doing that but know he is the only one who can persuade Mom to change her mind. Everything is on the line. He needs to know my side. Here is the CliffsNotes version of my two-page dramatic plea.

> *Dad, put yourself in my shoes.*
>
> *How would you feel?*
>
> *Can we at least do a trial to test?*
>
> *Talk with Mom. I will wait. Thank you.*
>
> *I love you. Your favorite oldest daughter who adores and respects you.*
>
> *~Amy*

WALK DEEPER

1. Have you ever written a note to share your thoughts?

    _____

    _____

    _____

2. Who do you recruit when you need help?_____

    _____

    _____

3. How does God go the extra mile with you? _____

    _____

    _____

MEMORY VERSE

"Pour out all your worries and stress upon him *and leave them there*, for he always tenderly cares for you."

—1 PETER 5:7 (TPT)

> *I pray to go the extra mile with you, God, in Jesus' name, Amen.*

DAY 5

AND LEAVE THEM THERE ...

The verdict is in. I hold my breath in anticipation. After much deliberation, I hear an unexpected *YES*! Oh my gosh.

This victory must be kept quiet. I remain calm. I understand it is a trial. Mom's not happy about loosening the reins and letting go of control. I thank Dad profusely for a chance to prove myself.

I shut my bedroom door and leap, throw my arms up in the air, whisper shout, and collapse with joy—all at the same time.

"For the record, I trust *you*, not other drivers," says Mom.

I promise all will be fine. They do trust me. I am so happy! In return, I have extra chores, babysitting, weeds, and more since I will have extra time. I will do it all. It is worth it to experience a new level of freedom.

WALK DEEPER

1. How does it feel when you are trusted with more?_____
    _____
    _____

2. Do you follow through and finish what is asked of you?
    _____
    _____
    _____

3. How does God celebrate victories with you? _____
    _____
    _____

MEMORY VERSE

"Pour out all your worries and stress upon him *and leave them there*, for he always tenderly cares for you."

—1 PETER 5:7 (TPT)

> *Thank you, God, that we already won, in Jesus' name, Amen.*

DAY 6

FOR HE ALWAYS...

A new world is opening. I get extra sleep, and I'm home earlier. This is refreshing! I do not even mind extra chores.

"The hunk of metal will do more damage to others if there happens to be an altercation," they say.

Driving to school is easy. My friend and I alternate days. Her car is sporty and fun. I drive a powder blue tanker, one of our gigantic "steel on wheels" family vehicles. Dad says Mom will worry less this way. *Just drive slowly and take your time.*

I can barely see over the dashboard. I feel like my grandma, but I do not care. If she can do it, so can I. Parking is a problem, so I find the farthest open spot—away from everything. On my driving days, this requires running to avoid a tardy slip.

I don't even care what I look like. "Steel on wheels" is better than the bus and gives Mom and Dad peace of mind.

WALK DEEPER

1. How do you handle extra freedom or time? _____
   _____
   _____

2. What do you take for granted?_____
   _____
   _____

3. Is it easy or hard to follow God's timing? Do you run
   ahead or wait? Share. _____
   _____
   _____

MEMORY VERSE

"Pour out all your worries and stress upon him *and leave them
there*, for he always tenderly cares for you."

—1 PETER 5:7 (TPT)

I pray to give thanks for new experiences, in Jesus' name, Amen.

DAY 7

TENDERLY CARES FOR YOU...

I am nominated for the senior football homecoming court. Secretly, I want to be crowned homecoming queen. I imagine myself waving while wearing the white sash and sparkling crown. Do not tell me you have not.

How silly. No one cares. I do though.

Everyone is silent as our names are called one by one to stand and be recognized. My heart is pounding out of my chest. I can barely hear—it is loud, and everything is pitch black. I hear over the loudspeaker: "And the runner-up, our senior home-coming attendant, is (please do not say my name) . . ." *Me.*

I hear my name, and the entire school immediately explodes in excitement for my friend as they hand me flowers. I return to my seat as they shine the spotlight and officially crown her queen.

I am happy for her. She deserves it. I smile but pretend not to be disappointed. How many votes did I lose? Was it close? No one knows.

Pathetic, right? How many would love to be in my shoes? I didn't feel good enough. It is time to let go of this ridiculous lie.

WALK DEEPER

1. How do you respond when you do not get what you
   want? _____

   _____

   _____

2. Do you genuinely celebrate others' successes? Share.

   _____

   _____

   _____

3. What does the crown God has just for you look like?

   _____

   _____

   _____

MEMORY VERSE

"Pour out all your worries and stress upon him *and leave them
there*, for he always tenderly cares for you."

—1 PETER 5:7 (TPT)

> *God, help me remember I am your royal daughter,*
> *in Jesus' name, Amen.*

LET GO

PRAYER

Thank you, Lord, for helping me to let go, especially when I do not want to. Forgive me for wanting to look in the rearview mirror. It is comfortable because it is what I know. That is not where I grow. Thank you for reminding me to live in the moment and appreciate what I have. Help me to let go of thoughts that are not from you and to hold every thought captive. I choose to let go of fear, striving, and comparison. Help me to let myself off the hook.

Your persistent and faithful daughter

Sweet daughter, let go of distractions. Focus on me. I will never let you go.

Your forever loving daddy,

God

LET GO

DECLARATIONS FROM GOD

Let go of fear.

Let go of shame.

Let go of doubt.

Let go of anxiety.

Let go of offense.

Let go of sadness.

Let go of complaining.

Let go of bitterness.

Let go of comparison.

Let go of resentment.

Let go of control.

Let go of yesterday.

Let go of worry.

Let go of your limiting beliefs.

WEEK 9

FLY WITH ME

MEMORY VERSE

"But those who trust in the Lord will find new strength.
They will soar high on wings like eagles.
They will run and not grow weary. They will walk and not faint."

—ISAIAH 40:31 (NLT)

DAY 1

BUT THOSE WHO TRUST IN THE LORD . . .

C ollege. Classmates cannot stop talking about it. The thought makes my head hurt. More school.

What do I want to be or do with my life? I am still figuring out who I am. I need more time.

I do not want to babysit forever or work in my parents' laundromat business. Dirty clothes? No thank you.

Cooking, cleaning, and hairstyling are off the list. My dolls never complain about their hair or clothes, but cutting my bangs when I was little ruined everything. Think zigzag. I can still taste soap in my mouth (my punishment for lying about cutting my hair).

I loved playing school in our basement. Maybe I could be a teacher? Not a nurse or real estate agent. Cannot handle throw-up or demanding clients.

Maybe a news anchor. Traveling the world reporting events sounds exciting. So many choices. What is best for me?

WALK DEEPER

1.   How do you handle decisions about your future? Is it easy or hard to hold your thoughts captive? Why or why not? __

     _____

     _____

2.   Do your thoughts consume you? Why or why not? Share how. _____

     _____

     _____

3.   How do you trust God when you have many choices?

     _____

     _____

     _____

MEMORY VERSE

"But those who trust in the Lord will find new strength.
They will soar high on wings like eagles.
They will run and not grow weary. They will walk and not faint."

—ISAIAH 40:31 (NLT)

> *I pray to live in my true identity you gave me, God,*
> *in Jesus' name, Amen.*

DAY 2

WILL FIND NEW STRENGTH...

My ACT (American College Testing) scores are not good. My GPA (grade point average—I knew that one) is average. I work hard and do my best but get mostly B's. I always get an A for effort.

B's are good grades for many. They scream disappointment for me because of the countless hours I spend studying. I know the material and cringe every time I see red marks.

I cannot figure out how many classmates breeze through and barely study. I do not give up and always complete my assignments. Why do I have to work twice as hard? Nothing is easy. Pressure builds. Maybe my expectations are off?

I'm a good girl but flopping like a fish out of water. I will not quit.

A NOTE FROM GOD

I see how hard you are working. Keep it up. I am proud of you. You are enough. I believe in you. I am inside of you. It is not what you see; it is what you do not (2 Corinthians 5:7). Trust me. You are not a failure or disappointment. Come higher. With me. I will show you the truth. Trust me.

I will not let you fall,

God

WALK DEEPER

1. How do you handle pressure? _____
    _____
    _____

2. Do you struggle with comparison or perfectionism?
    Share._____
    _____
    _____

3. How does God give you strength? _____
    _____
    _____

MEMORY VERSE

"But those who trust in the Lord will find new strength.
They will soar high on wings like eagles.
They will run and not grow weary. They will walk and not faint."

—ISAIAH 40:31 (NLT)

*I pray to rely on your strength, God, and not on my own,
in Jesus' name, Amen.*

DAY 3

THEY WILL SOAR HIGH...

My scores confirm I do not measure up. I am overthinking everything. We visit colleges in and out of state. I am going through the motions checking off requirements. I'm overwhelmed.

My high school counselor does not help. Or does she? Her words fire something in me. I think of all the times in the past when people doubted me, and a determination rises up to succeed, no matter what. It is not what she can see in my scores that matters—it is what she does not see in my character, grit, and determination that allows my wings to spread and soar.

NAOMI & RUTH

Naomi and her husband did not know what to do during the famine, so they left Bethlehem and moved to the land of Moab. Naomi had two sons who found wives there. Shortly after, Naomi's husband and two sons sadly died. Naomi felt exceedingly small and unimportant.

Naomi decided she would go back to Bethlehem. One of her daughters-in-law clung to Naomi and said, "Where you go, I go. Your people will be my people and your God will be my God." Her name was Ruth (Ruth 1:16).

Naomi and Ruth set out for Bethlehem. They did not know it, but God was taking care of them. God knew their hearts were sad and life was hard. He prepared a way for them.

In Bethlehem, Ruth needed to collect food for herself and Naomi. She went to a field and picked up grain that had fallen to the ground. The owner of the field asked his workers, "Who is this woman?" Ruth did not realize the owner of the field was Boaz, a relative of Naomi.

Boaz saw Ruth as a good worker who cared for Naomi. Boaz was kind to Ruth and invited her for a meal. He also sent her home with grain. Naomi was grateful Ruth found the field of Boaz. "May he be blessed by the Lord," Naomi said.

Naomi wanted Ruth to be taken care of. She sent her to where Boaz was sleeping. "Who are you?" Boaz asked when he realized somebody was there.

"It is Ruth," she said.

Boaz was honored Ruth was willing to marry him, but there was a closer relative to her than him. Boaz went to town to meet the relative who said he could not take care of Ruth. God knew Boaz would show kindness to Ruth and Naomi. The relative gave Boaz permission to marry Ruth.

Naomi and Ruth felt small, but God could see them. God knew what they needed, prepared their way, and took care of them. Soon God blessed Ruth and Boaz with a son (Ruth 4:14–15).

God already knows where I am going to college. He is preparing the way. I simply need to do the work and fill out applications.

WALK DEEPER

1. Do you overthink? Share. _____
    _____
    _____

2. Who are trusted advisors in your life? How do they help
    guide you? _____
    _____
    _____

3. How is God faithful with you when you feel small?_____
    _____
    _____

MEMORY VERSE

"But those who trust in the Lord will find new strength.
They will soar high on wings like eagles.
They will run and not grow weary. They will walk and not faint."

—ISAIAH 40:31 (NLT)

I pray to soar with you and your words, God, in Jesus' name, Amen.

DAY 4

ON WINGS LIKE EAGLES...

We are reviewing my school records. My counselor is shaking her head. "You'll be lucky to get into *any* school, let alone any of *these* schools."

I am numb, holding back tears, and completely blindsided. My mind races for a thought that makes sense. I do not remember anything she says next but leave determined.

A private all-girls school is my top choice.

How could she say that? How unkind, let alone unprofessional. My scores are not a reflection of me. If I came this far, I can continue.

Flashbacks of summer tutoring, additional daily help, and hours of extra studying come flooding in. I've worked hard. I've shown up, completed everything asked of me, and not slacked or given up, even when I wanted to.

I choose to disregard my counselor's comment. I feel like I just got kicked out of the nest. It is time to spread my wings and fly. I have grit.

> **Grit:** a firmness of mind; invincible spirit;
> unyielding courage or fearlessness; fortitude.
>
> —Yourdictionary.com

WALK DEEPER

1. How do you respond when you get a bad report? _____
    _____
    _____

2. Are you able to let unfavorable words or advice go?
    Share._____
    _____
    _____

3. What fearlessness did God put inside of you?_____
    _____
    _____

MEMORY VERSE

"But those who trust in the Lord will find new strength.
They will soar high on wings like eagles.
They will run and not grow weary. They will walk and not faint."

—ISAIAH 40:31 (NLT)

I pray for your purpose in my life to be filled, in Jesus' name, Amen.

DAY 5

"How did the meeting with your counselor go?"

"Great, and I am all set. I just need to submit my applications," I tell Mom. Otherwise, she will be in the school office faster than lightning, demanding an apology as well as an explanation.

I think back to my brother's freshman basketball tryouts when he was the only one cut. He was crushed, and I could hear him crying through my bedroom wall all night long. My heart ached for my brother, wishing I could take away the pain, but I knew he had to go through it. Mom drove to school the next day and spoke to the coach, who happened to be our dean of students, demanding to know what he was thinking cutting only one player.

Some things are better left alone. I know my mother would jump into action if I needed her, but this battle is mine to fly *through* not from. I am drawing the line in the sand.

I WILL STATEMENTS

I will go to college.
I will earn a degree.
I will succeed.
I will continue to learn.
I will not be held back.
I will persist.
I will be the best I can be.
I will finish what I start.
I will break through.
I will spread my wings and fly.
I will put one foot in front of the other.
I will walk.
I will be brave.
I will be ME.
Nothing will hold me back, even others' remarks.

WALK DEEPER

1. Do you share everything you are thinking? Explain. _____
   _____
   _____

2. What declarations have you made for yourself? _____
   _____
   _____

3. How does God fight for you?_____
   _____
   _____

MEMORY VERSE

"But those who trust in the Lord will find new strength.
They will soar high on wings like eagles.
They will run and not grow weary. They will walk and not faint."

—ISAIAH 40:31 (NLT)

I pray to run with you, God, despite the odds, in Jesus' name, Amen.

DAY 6

AND NOT GROW WEARY...

For weeks I volunteer daily to check the mailbox. Finally, envelopes start trickling in. I am accepted letter after letter to every college I apply to. I am ecstatic! Perseverance pays off.

Now I cannot decide which one. Dad creates a brilliant plan. He knows colleges are businesses wanting money. I am emotional and indecisive. Dad presents a spreadsheet and asks me to review it.

"Your grandfather always wanted to go to college," Dad says. "He did not have the opportunity. His dad died young, leaving him to support the family. He worked and paid for both of his sisters' higher education, sacrificing his dream. Nothing will please him more than to see his oldest grandchild carry the gift of college forward."

I am speechless. I realize how special it is to continue my education. I get to fulfill my grandpa's dream right in front of him. I will soar.

WALK DEEPER

1. When have you applied for something not knowing the results? Share. _____

    _____

    _____

2. How have you or your family made sacrifices? _____

    _____

    _____

3. Who in your family has God assigned to guide you? Who are you to be guiding? Share. _____

    _____

    _____

MEMORY VERSE

"But those who trust in the Lord will find new strength.
They will soar high on wings like eagles.
They will run and not grow weary. They will walk and not faint."

—ISAIAH 40:31 (NLT)

*I pray to not grow weary and to rest in you, God,
in Jesus' name, Amen.*

DAY 7
THEY WILL WALK AND NOT FAINT . . .

My heart pounds as I scan Dad's homemade spreadsheet left to right, up and down. Dad has my accepted colleges listed across the top—most expensive to least expensive, left to right. All fees and expenses are showing, along with what Mom and Dad will contribute. Education is important but not free. I know I paid half for high school.

My eyes go to the bottom of each column, where Dad has shown the amount I am expected to contribute. Most schools will require I take out a loan to pay for tuition. I start calculating in my head how much I will need to work to avoid taking out a loan, until my eyes find the last column of the spreadsheet. Way at the end, in the bottom right-hand corner, I see zero dollars. No college loan necessary. What?!

"Sleep on it. You choose," they say. I know my answer before bed.

I bounce downstairs in the morning to share my decision. Above the signature line is a paragraph around the decision stating if I quit, fail, or get kicked out, I am required to pay my parents back in full. Plus interest.

I am responsible for books, miscellaneous fees, and spending money. Graduating with zero debt? You bet I will be. This is awesome! Without hesitation and complete confidence, I sign and date, agreeing to Mom and Dad's terms.

I will officially be leaving the nest. It is time to spread my wings and fly on my own for the first time.

WALK DEEPER

1. Do you make decisions quickly or take your time? Explain. _____

   _____

   _____

2. How do you feel when you are confident about a decision?_____

   _____

   _____

3. Do you ask God and wait, or do you tend to run ahead? Share._____

   _____

   _____

MEMORY VERSE

"But those who trust in the Lord will find new strength.
They will soar high on wings like eagles.
They will run and not grow weary. They will walk and not faint."

—ISAIAH 40:31 (NLT)

> *I pray to stay in step with you, God, in Jesus' name, Amen.*

FLY WITH ME

PRAYER

Thank you for reminding me to trust you for everything. I ask for your supernatural strength. Help me not rely on my strength so I do not get tired. Thank you that I get to walk with you.

Your fearless daughter

Sweet daughter, I am your wings. Let me show you.
Fly with me.

Your forever loving daddy,

God

FLY WITH ME

DECLARATIONS FROM GOD

Fly with me nonstop.
Fly with me willingly.
Fly with me passionately.
Fly with me anticipating more.
Fly with me higher.
Fly with me courageously.
Fly with me without hesitation.
Fly with me boldly.
Fly with me uninhibited.
Fly with me boundless.
Fly with me beautifully.
Fly with me creatively.
Fly with me not looking back.
Fly with me forever.

WEEK 10

YOU CAN

MEMORY VERSE

"And Jesus said to him, 'If you can!
All things are possible for one who believes.'"

—MARK 9:23 (ESV)

DAY 1

AND JESUS...

College-bound?! I am on top of the world. I cannot believe I have a roommate lined up. I know, right?!

"You want to room together?" I ask our homecoming queen.

"That would be awesome," she says.

I feel a little weird, as I do not know her well, but heard she did not have anyone lined up. She does not hesitate, and both of us are relieved.

One less decision, and I do not have to live with a stranger. I am proud of myself. I mean *really proud of myself*, for one of the first times in my life—especially since I did not let my school counselor deter me. She did not believe in me, but I did.

I can do this.

WALK DEEPER

1.   Share a time you were proud of yourself. _____
     _____
     _____

2.   What can you do when you make up your mind? _____
     _____
     _____

3.   How can God help you? Share. _____
     _____
     _____

MEMORY VERSE

"And Jesus said to him, 'If you can!
All things are possible for one who believes.'"

—MARK 9:23 (ESV)

I pray to be proud of myself, in Jesus' name, Amen.

DAY 2

SAID TO HIM...

The last year of high school. How is it possible? It is fun, fast, and at times a blur. We wrap up our final assignments and projects. Everything is flowing, and spring is approaching. So is change.

One of my final classes requires me to serve in the community. I will never forget the nursing home. It smells like a hospital but feels like a nursery. The staff is nice, organized, and everything is clean but does not feel like home. Many are sitting alone and cannot do simple things by themselves.

We are each assigned to one resident. My heart aches for Ida. I sit and help her eat her lunch, wiping her mouth while she shares about her life. She is a widow but loves her son who lives in Ithaca, New York.

Ida lights up every time she sees me. Our time together is special. I smile and listen. She reminds me to enjoy the journey and not to take anything for granted.

I vow to remain humble. Life is a gift.

WALK DEEPER

1. Do you like serving? Share. _____
   _____
   _____

2. How do you describe your heart? Is it easy to be
   humble? _____
   _____
   _____

3. Why does God bring people in and out of your life?____
   _____
   _____

MEMORY VERSE

"And Jesus said to him, 'If you can!
All things are possible for one who believes.'"

—MARK 9:23 (ESV)

> *I pray to remain humble in you, God, in Jesus' name, Amen.*

DAY 3

IF YOU CAN …

P rom is beyond what I imagined. Mom and I shop for weeks, and we find the perfect dress, agreeing as soon as I slip it on. Silver, sequins, stylish, simple. Perfect fit and price. We will take this one!

New shiny heels and matching jewelry complete my outfit. Hair done, nails painted, lipstick on. I can dress up like a princess. I finally feel beautiful—after so many years of awkwardly trying to be like everyone else but being treated like an unwanted stepsister.

Pictures are fun, dinner delicious, and we end up dancing with no shoes. Heels hurt after a while! The atmosphere is magical with white-covered tables, china, candles, and flower centerpieces. My classmates all look amazing, and everyone's on their best behavior.

My cheeks hurt. I cannot stop smiling ear to ear with my perfect, bonded front teeth showing. What a fairytale.

WALK DEEPER

1.   Do you like dressing up? Formal or informal? Share.____
     _____
     _____

2.   What makes you smile? _____
     _____
     _____

3.   How does God make you feel like a princess?_____
     _____
     _____

MEMORY VERSE

"And Jesus said to him, 'If you can!
All things are possible for one who believes.'"

—MARK 9:23 (ESV)

> *I pray to be your princess, God, in Jesus' name, Amen.*

DAY 4

ALL THINGS...

I feel like I am on cruise control. Can we put on the brakes? It seems like yesterday I was climbing off the yellow school bus. Now I am getting fitted for my graduation cap and gown.

The final months are filled with graduation practice, cleaning lockers, signing yearbooks, and celebrating each other's accomplishments. We laugh at the most likely to flirt, have a party, be out of uniform, succeed, get married, or more at the end of the yearbook. All candidates are spot on. Excitement is in the air.

Baccalaureate is done. Commencement is over. I move my tassel.

We give farewell wishes and hugs. Will I see some again? I hope so but have a feeling I may not. It makes me sad knowing some of our paths may never cross again.

Just like that, another chapter closes.

NEHEMIAH

King Artaxerxes noticed Nehemiah looked sad. He asked him why. Nehemiah told the king, "The city where my people lived has been destroyed and gates are torn down." The king asked Nehemiah what he wanted to do.

Nehemiah prayed and asked God what to say to the king. Then he said, "Please let me go home and rebuild Jerusalem's wall and gates." The king wanted to help Nehemiah, so he allowed him to go to Jerusalem to work to repair the city. He even helped Nehemiah get supplies.

When Nehemiah returned to Jerusalem, he rode around the city to see what needed to be done. Then he told the people he had returned to rebuild its wall and gates. He also told them he would need lots of help.

In fifty-two days, the wall and gates were finished. The people celebrated and worshiped God because now they had a secure wall and strong gates around their city.

Nehemiah was no longer sad, but thankful God used him to help do this important work.

God always uses people to accomplish His purposes. When I trust God, I can do all things, even if it seems impossible. I can successfully finish high school. I can apply and get into college. I can pass the baton, telling younger classmates to appreciate every moment—because they can.

WALK DEEPER

1. Do you live in the moment? Share how._____

   _____

   _____

2. Do you take advantage of all things in front of you? ____

   _____

   _____

3. How does God specifically equip you? _____

   _____

   _____

MEMORY VERSE

"And Jesus said to him, 'If you can!
All things are possible for one who believes.'"

—MARK 9:23 (ESV)

I pray to not rush, in Jesus' name, Amen.

DAY 5

"Friends shift, so appreciate the moments. Nothing lasts forever," says Mom. I thought she was wrong; she is not.

I do not like when relationships end. I cannot stand good-byes. I love people—even the mean ones, which is odd. I hope for the best. Many faces, from elementary school, middle school, and now high school, I will never see again.

Some disappear, while others stick. There is often no rhyme or reason, just a flow in and out. Is it something I said or did not say? I am always second-guessing myself. Doors shut and new ones open. Some relationships end while others blossom.

I think of all the weeds I voluntarily pulled as a kid, choosing fresh air and sunshine over cooking and doing dishes. And that's still true! I specialized in helping my dad make the weeds disappear so they wouldn't take over our gravel driveway or backyard. No way would we let them choke out our flowers, shrubs, and grass. Plus, weeds just look bad. I know several things and people in my life need to be pulled out in order for me to grow stronger, but it's not always easy.

Pruning. Is there any other way?

WALK DEEPER

1. How do you handle goodbyes? _____
    _____
    _____

2. Do you know when doors are opening and shutting?
    Share. _____
    _____
    _____

3. Why does God prune you? Are you aware? _____
    _____
    _____

MEMORY VERSE

"And Jesus said to him, 'If you can!
All things are possible for one who believes.'"

—MARK 9:23 (ESV)

I pray to walk through your doors, God, in Jesus' name, Amen.

DAY 6

We spend the summer celebrating our accomplishments. We attend one graduation party after the next, laughing, reminiscing, and dreaming out loud. Parties slowly fade, and the countdown begins. I feel a shift from looking back to looking forward.

Can I do this? Can I leave my family? Can I be responsible on my own?

> **Faith:** complete trust or confidence in someone or something: belief that is not based on proof; belief in God or the doctrines or teachings of religion; belief in anything, as a code of ethics, standards of merit, etc.; a system of religious belief; the obligation of loyalty or fidelity to a person, promise, engagement, etc.
>
> —Dictionary.com

I can do this. I can leave my family. I can be responsible on my own.

I can walk by faith if I keep my eye on the ball (*pssst*, God). Not to my left, right, infield, or outfield. Helmet on, bat in hand, grip loose, arms lifted, breathing calm, eyes focused, heart open, and stance firm yet soft.

Wait for the right pitch. Trust when to swing, making contact. Block out the noise.

A NOTE FROM GOD

Yes, you can. You are ready and responsible. You can because you have me. Continue to persevere. You will not fail, and you are not alone (Deuteronomy 31:8). You are mine. The journey is long, but you can endure. I am with you in the highs and lows, twists and turns, detours, differing speeds, mistakes, and victories. Lean back on my guardrails and never stop asking me for help. Trust me so you can soar like countless times before. You will fall, but I will help you up. Dream bigger and expect miracles. Put one foot in front of the other when you do not know what is next. It is time for an increase in faith, sweet daughter.

You can,

God

WALK DEEPER

1. Share how you celebrated a win in your life. _____
    _____
    _____

2. Do you have faith you can do what you put your mind
    to? Share. _____
    _____
    _____

3. How does God block the noise in your life? _____
    _____
    _____

MEMORY VERSE

"And Jesus said to him, 'If you can!
All things are possible for one who believes.'"

—MARK 9:23 (ESV)

I pray to walk by faith, not by sight, in Jesus' name, Amen.

DAY 7

A volleyball tries to take me out—at my own high school graduation party! I wish I were joking, but I am not.

My friends and I are playing in my backyard. We are having the best time! Out of nowhere, the ball slams into my face, a serve from the opposing team. My head snaps back.

Thankfully, I am able to hide my tears. It is pitch black. I am not sure why I am laughing, saying, "I'm fine," while seeing stars and the moon. Literally. Now that's talent.

I gasp while quickly reaching my hand to my mouth. No! Please do not tell me I broke my front tooth again. Phew, my teeth are all intact. I sigh in relief, yet I am in excruciating pain.

Back to the dentist I go. Mom knows the number by heart. They do another root canal in the other front tooth but thankfully nothing else. I handle the dentist chair, shots, procedure, and numbness like a champ. In and out.

I now know I can get through anything. I can celebrate and have fun, but things are not ever going to be perfect. I trust you, God, no matter what.

I cannot be sidelined.

WALK DEEPER

1. Have you ever been taken out by something unexpected? _____

   _____

   _____

2. How do you feel when you are sidelined? _____

   _____

   _____

3. How does God help you get through all things? Share.

   _____

   _____

   _____

MEMORY VERSE

"And Jesus said to him, 'If you can!
All things are possible for one who believes.'"

—MARK 9:23 (ESV)

I pray to not play it safe, in Jesus' name, Amen.

YOU CAN

PRAYER

Thank you for reminding me to place my confidence in you. I can do what I put my mind to if I choose you. I ask for your supernatural strength. Help me not rely on my own so I do not get tired or give up too soon. I am available and ask you to put me in the game. Help me not back down in fear. Use me. I can and choose to play on your team.

Your fearless daughter

Sweet daughter, do not discount what I put in you. You can. All you need is in you. Be curious.

Your forever loving daddy,

God

YOU CAN

DECLARATIONS FROM GOD

You can do anything with me.
You can overcome it.
You can believe me.
You can hear me.
You can look for me.
You can feel me.
You can praise me.
You can expect more.
You can talk to me.
You can transform.
You can trust me.
You can push through.
You can finish.
You can love because I love you.

ACKNOWLEDGMENTS

Mom and Dad, you're simply the best parents. Thank you for being a great example of what love looks like. Thank you for always showing up, rain or shine. Thank you for loving, protecting, pushing, and preparing me. Thank you for showing me the ropes, paving the way, and fighting for me when I didn't know how. I love you both more than you know. Thank you, God, for personally choosing John and Kathy to steward me.

Without my husband, Bob, this book wouldn't exist. Thank you for your belief, support, encouragement, and investment. Thank you for making me write out a detailed business plan, including a cost analysis (still not sure how I passed, but let's be honest—you love me). Thank you for reminding me multiple times there is no turning back, that I can do this, and to finish strong. Your yes continues to bless me beyond words.

Thank you, Charlotte, Vivian, Penelope, Mattie, Joanie, Sarah, Debbie and family for taking time to read the unpolished manuscript. Thank you for your honest feedback and insight that helped smooth many rough edges. You cheered me on in more ways than you'll ever know. I'm humbled and grateful.

Janet, thank you for loving me through the first round of editing. The original writing was wordy, scattered, and just plain bad. No, seriously, it was. You gracefully guided me and even tried to get me to fire you. I didn't. Heck, looking back, I would have fired me. Thank you for helping me officially start.

Melanie, thank you for cheering me on, interceding and praying for a publisher when I asked you to. Within twenty-four hours you texted me with your friend Beth's contact information, saying, "I had no idea she was an editor and publisher. Check out her website and see what you think." The rest is history.

Beth Lottig of Inspire Books, you are the best book coach and publishing consultant a hopeful novice writer could hope for. God knew who and what I needed to bring this work to life. Thank you for genuinely challenging me to rewrite the entire manuscript with a different focus. I was not thrilled, but am glad I listened and did it again. Thank you for your expertise, patience, diligence, and heartfelt engagement throughout this process.

Thank you also for recommending Melinda Martin, Martin Publishing Services. Melinda, I knew from our first meeting you would over-deliver and not miss a detail. Thank you for creatively pulling this all together and for rejecting many of my ideas. Yours are way better. The proof is in the pudding!

Thank you, Victoria Leigh Images, for capturing and creating incredible photos. We rescheduled multiple times due to weather but finally connected one beautiful crisp evening. I'll never forget shivering, laughing, smiling, jumping, walking, sitting, and chatting with you in between. You were breathless as your camera clicked away in your mud boots and coat. Thank you for making me feel like a princess and straightening my crown. I'll never forget how you made me feel that hour. If you need a photographer, Vicki is your girl. She will go above and beyond your wildest expectations to help you see through a different lens.

And to Jesus, the true Author. Thank you for encouraging me to write. I'm sorry I pretended not to hear you ask me for almost three years. Please forgive me. The nudging became so intense I finally shouted, "Fine, I'll do it, but I don't know what I'm doing! This is scary." You answered, "Just pick up your pen, Amy. We'll do this together." Thank you for pursuing me. Thank you for making a way when I didn't see one or know what to do next. Thank you for whispering, "Just walk," on many occasions. Thank you for leading the way, showing me exactly where to step. I love walking hand in hand with you. Let's keep walking together!

ABOUT THE AUTHOR

AMY S. DUDLEY

Amy S. Dudley lives in Medina, Ohio, with her incredible husband, Bob, and their four children. She is an energetic, passionate author, speaker, leader, prayer warrior, Jesus lover, WARshipper, and fitness enthusiast who loves to laugh, encourage, read, travel, serve, and give. Amy's greatest ambitions are to love the lost and broken to freedom, but most importantly spending precious time with her family growing daily as an honorable, submitted, gracious, loving wife and mom. For more, check out AmySDudley.com.

Walk it out with us on the following platforms.

Instagram: @Amy.S.Dudley
Facebook: AmyMcCueDudley

Text the word WALK to 13305831956
to join our Walk It Out community.

j

Made in United States
Orlando, FL
10 December 2021